Collingwood Ontario in Colour Photos, Saving Our History One Photo at a Time

Photography
by Barbara Raué
2013

Series Name:
Cruising Ontario

Book 188: Collingwood

Cover photo: 185 Third Street, Page 19

Series Name: Cruising Ontario
Saving Our History One Photo at a Time
in colour photos

Books Available in Alphabetical Order:
Aberfoyle, Acton, Alton, Amherstburg, Ancaster, Arthur, Aylmer, Ayr, Bloomingdale, Brantford, Burlington, Caledon, Caledonia, Cambridge, Clifford, Conestogo, Delhi, Dorchester to Aylmer, Drayton, Drumbo, Dundas, Eden Mills, Elmira, Elora, Essex, Fergus, Guelph, Hagersville, Hamilton, Hanover, Harriston, Hespeler, Jarvis, Kingston, Kingsville, Kitchener, Linwood, Listowel, London, Lucknow, Mono, Mount Forest, Neustadt, New Hamburg, Niagara-on-the-Lake, Oakville, Orangeville, Orillia, Owen Sound, Palmerston, Peterborough, Petrolia, Port Elgin, Preston, Rockwood, Sarnia, Seaforth, Sheffield, Shelburne, Simcoe, Southampton, St. Jacobs, St. Marys, St. Thomas, Stoney Creek, Stratford, Thamesford, Tillsonburg, Waterdown, Waterford, Waterloo, Welland, Wellesley, Windsor, Wingham, Woodstock

Book 157: Brockville
Book 158: Merrickville
Book 159: Smiths Falls
Book 160: Portland, Newboro
Book 161: Westport & Area
Book 162: Perth
Book 163-166: Belleville
Book 167-168: Port Colborne
Book 169: Erin in Colour
Book 170: Goderich in Colour
Book 171: Sault Ste. Marie
Book 172: Lake Superior
Book 173-176: Thunder Bay
Book 177-179: Paris

Book 180: St. George
Book 182-183: Burford
Book 184: Mt Pleasant, Onondaga, Newport
Book 185-186: Grimsby
Book 187: Toronto in Colour
Book 188: Collingwood Colour

Other Books by Barbara Raue

Coins of Gold

Arrows, Indians and Love

The Life and Times of Barbara
Volume 1: Inventions That Have Enhanced My Life
Volume 2: Entertainment That I Have Enjoyed
Volume 3: East Coast Trips
Volume 4: Olympics Have Always Intrigued Me
Volume 5: Wonders of the World
Volume 6: Caribbean Cruises We Have Enjoyed
Volume 7: Animals
Volume 8: Storms and Other Major Disasters in My Lifetime
Volume 9: Wars, Terrorist Attacks and Major Disasters

The Cromwell Family Book

Laura Secord Discovered

Daddy Where Are You?

Montana Series
Book 1: Montana Dream
Book 2: Life on the Montana Frontier
Book 3: Montana to Boston and Back
Book 4: Montana Sons Go to War
Book 5: Montana Sons Return from War

Visit Barbara's website to view all of her books
http://barbararaue.ca

Collingwood is situated on Nottawasaga Bay at the southern point of Georgian Bay. Collingwood offers a combination of old time charm and history with recreation opportunities for skiing on Blue Mountain, and golfing.

Collingwood was incorporated as a town in 1858, nine years before Confederation and was named after Admiral Lord Cuthbert Collingwood, Lord Nelson's second in command at the Battle of Trafalgar, who assumed command of the British fleet after Nelson's death.

The land in the area was originally inhabited by the Iroquoian Petun nation, which built a string of villages in the vicinity of the nearby Niagara Escarpment. They were driven from the region by the Iroquois in 1650. European settlers and freed black slaves arrived in the area in the 1840s, bringing with them their religion and culture.

In 1855, the Ontario, Simcoe & Huron (later called The Northern) railway came into Collingwood, and the harbour became the place for shipment of goods destined for the upper Great Lakes ports of Chicago and Port Arthur-Ft. William (now Thunder Bay). Shipping produced a need for ship repairs, so it was not long before an organized ship building business was created. On May 24, 1883, the Collingwood Shipyards, formerly known as Collingwood Dry Dock Shipbuilding and Foundry Company Limited, opened with a special ceremony. On September 12, 1901, the Huronic was launched in Collingwood, the first steel-hulled ship launched in Canada. The shipyards produced Lakers and during World War II contributed to the production of Corvettes for the Royal Canadian Navy. Shipbuilding was one of the principal industries in the town, employing as much as 10% of the total labour force. Overseas competition and over capacity in shipbuilding in Canada led to the demise of shipbuilding in Collingwood in September 1986.

Collingwood attracted eleven new manufacturing firms by 1971. Eight additional manufacturing companies located here by 1983, making Collingwood the largest industrial employer in the region.

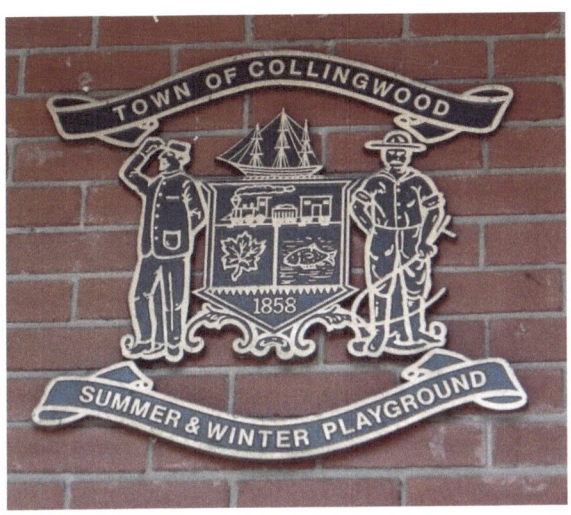

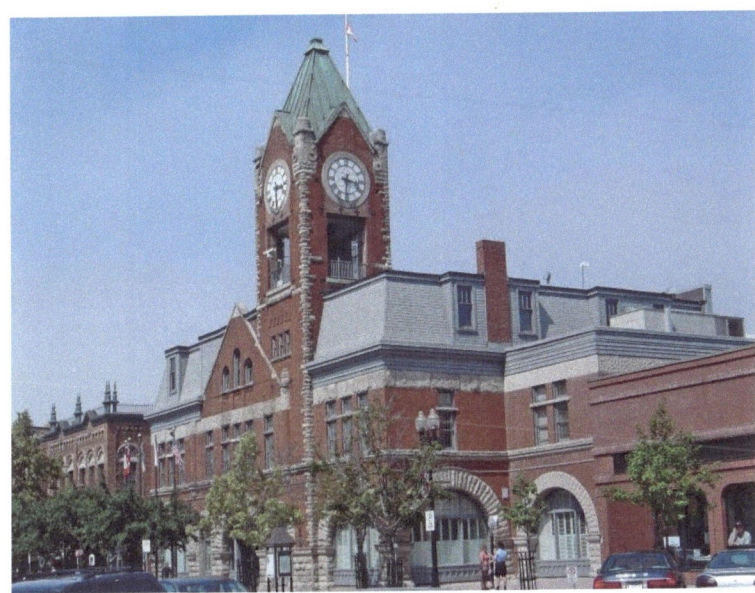

Clock tower

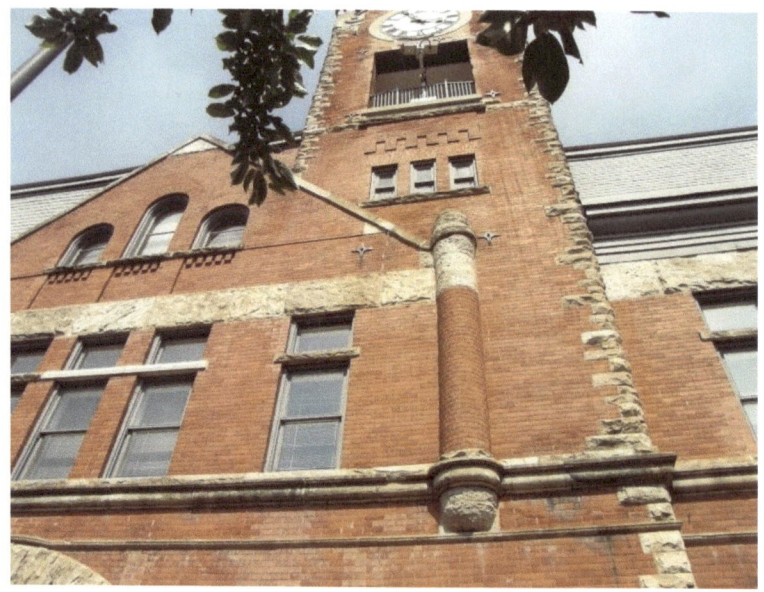
Corner quoins

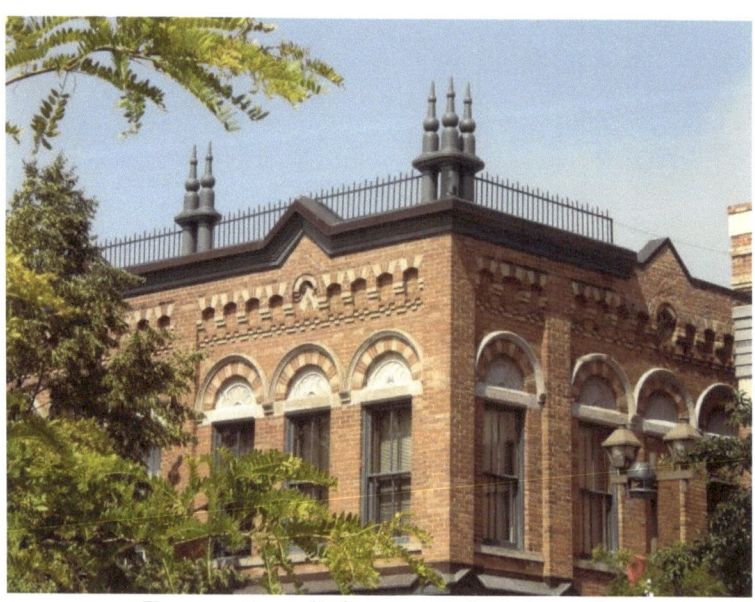
Decorative dichromatic brickwork

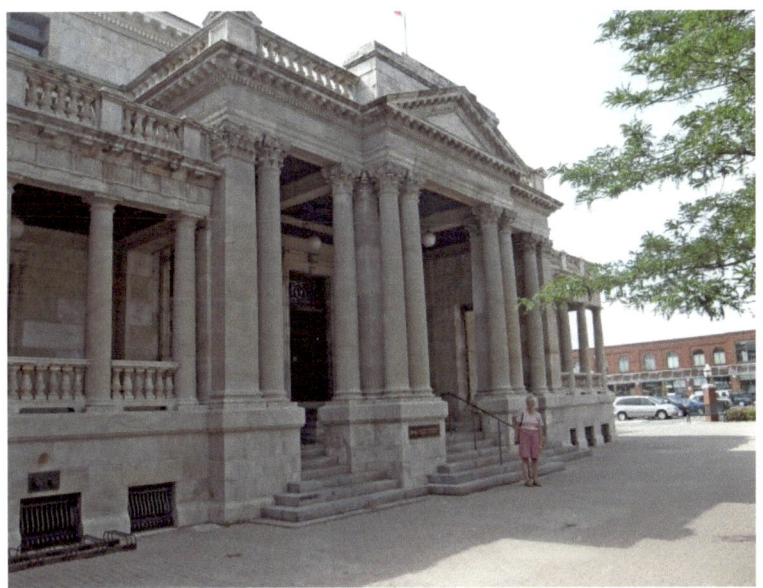

Government of Canada building – parapets, Corinthian and Doric columns, pediment, dentil molding, cornice brackets

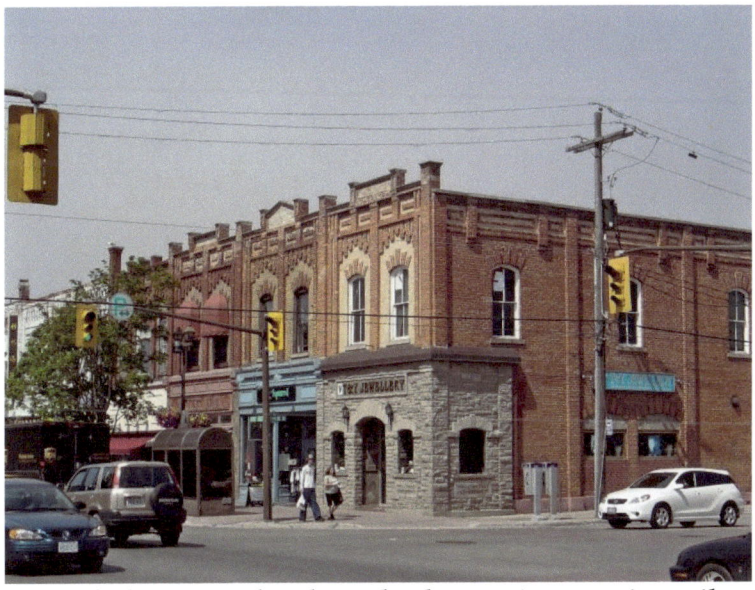

Parapet, dichromatic brickwork, decorative cornice, pilasters

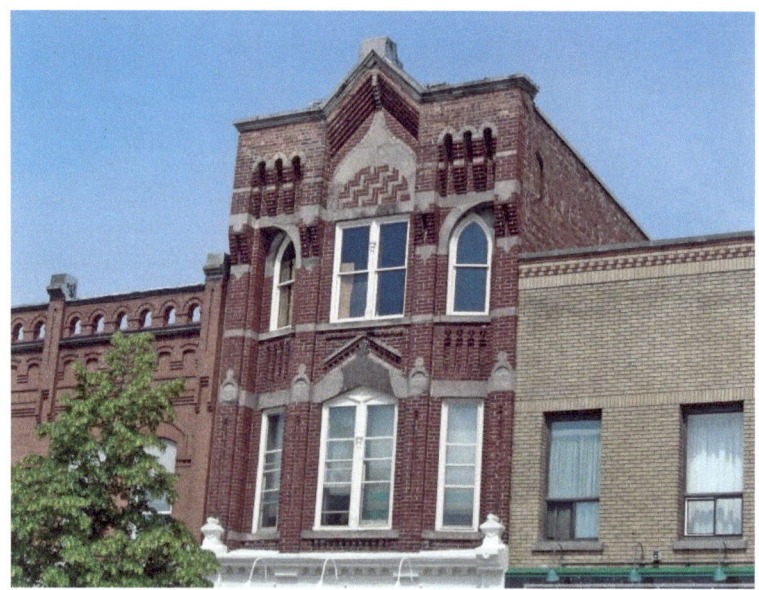
Three-bay façade, dichromatic brickwork

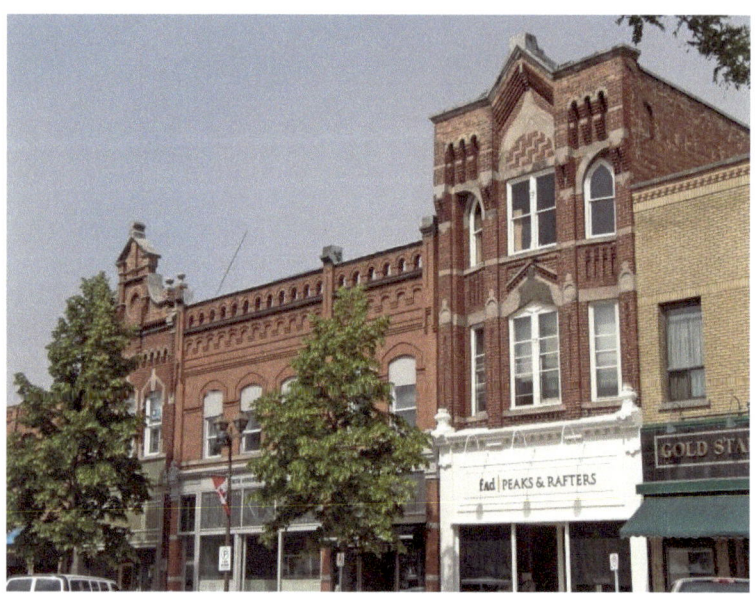
Bevelled dentil molding

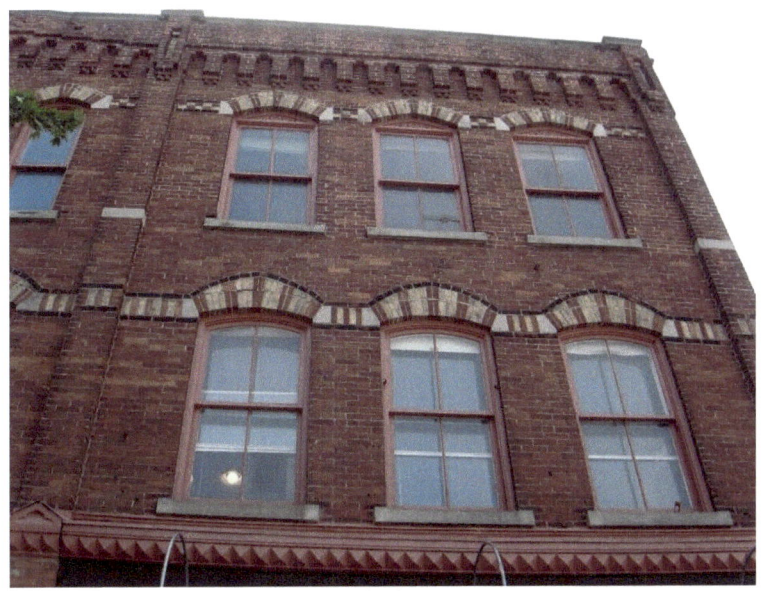
Dentil moulding, dichromatic voussoirs

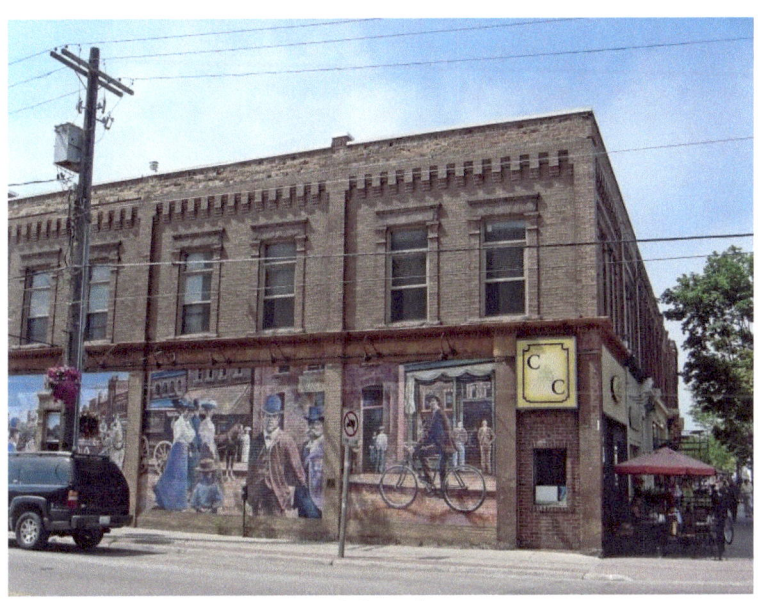
Mural

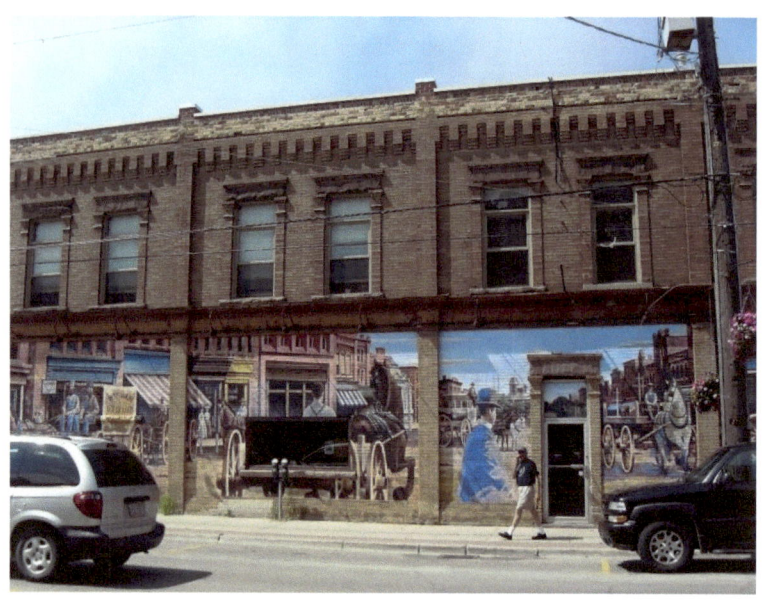

Murals

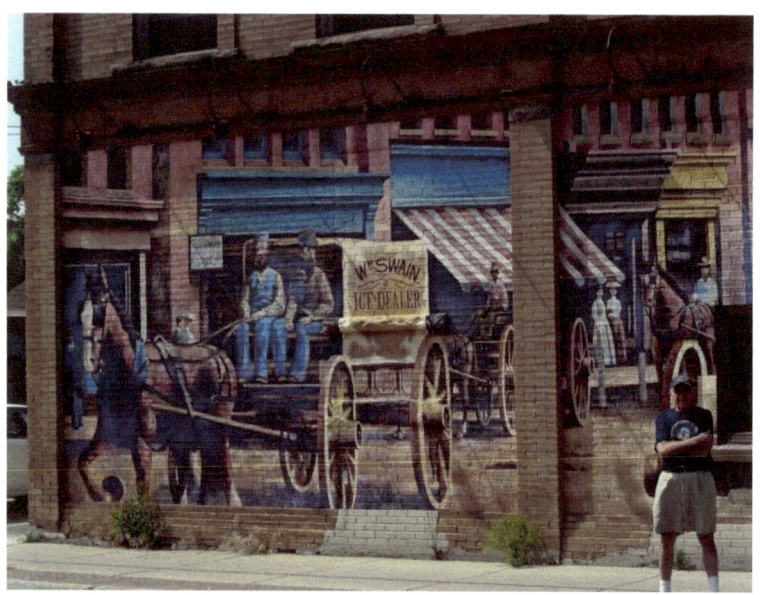

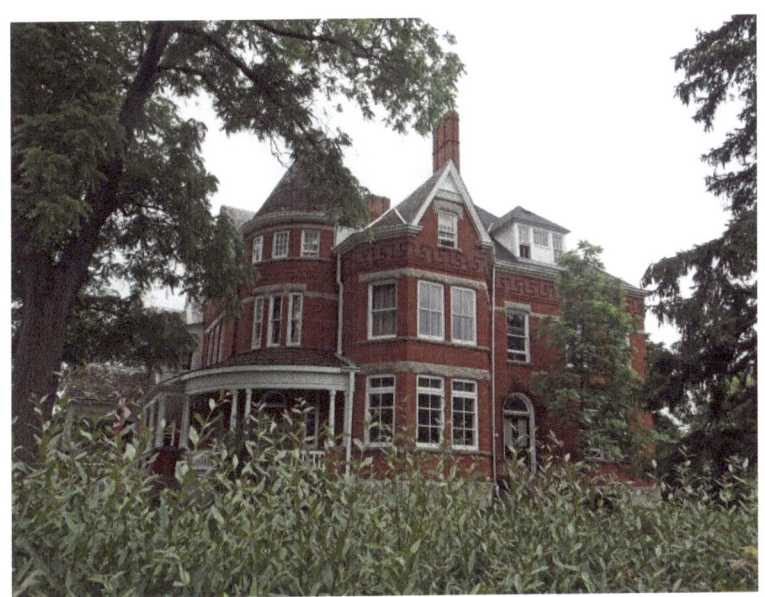

200 Oak Street - This 10,380 square foot Victorian home, the largest and tallest in Collingwood, at the corner of Oak and Third Streets was originally owned by Frank F. Telfer, a leading businessman and ex-mayor of Collingwood. He purchased the property in 1891, and by 1893 the local firm Bryan Brothers Manufacturing Company completed the construction of the Telfer home. In 1925 the Telfer family sold the house, and the "Gowans Home for Missionaries' Children" was established by the Interior Sudan Mission.

This home displays a variety of architectural features. The three storey structure is of double brick construction laid in a stretcher bond fashion and rests on a cut stone foundation. The three main exterior walls are accented by a repeating Greek style pattern running the full width of the walls below the eaves. The northeast corner of the building is formed by a large round turret with a conical roof. There are eighty windows of various shapes set above limestone sills; they include round, oriel, semicircular, and oval as well as stained glass.

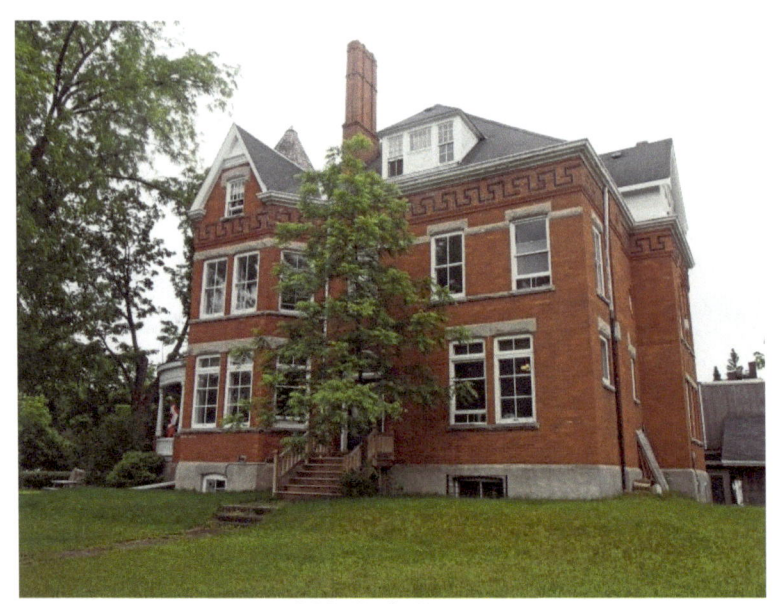

200 Oak Street

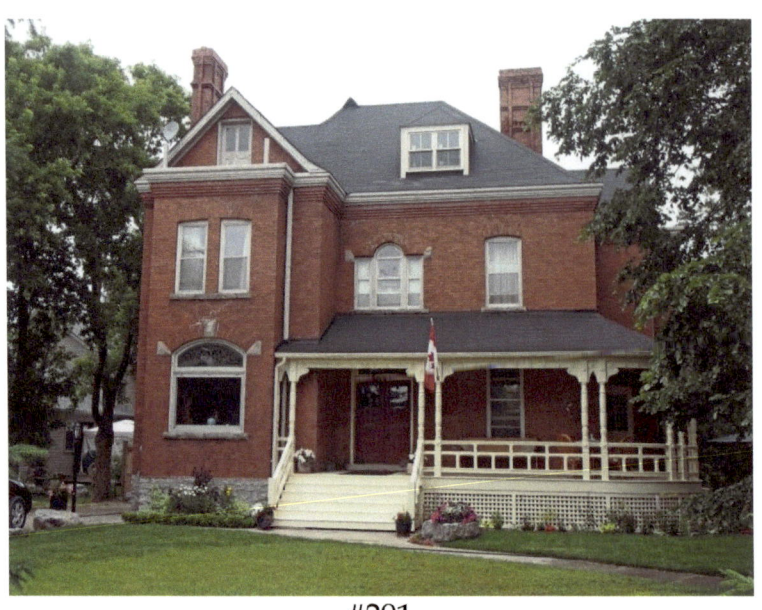

#291

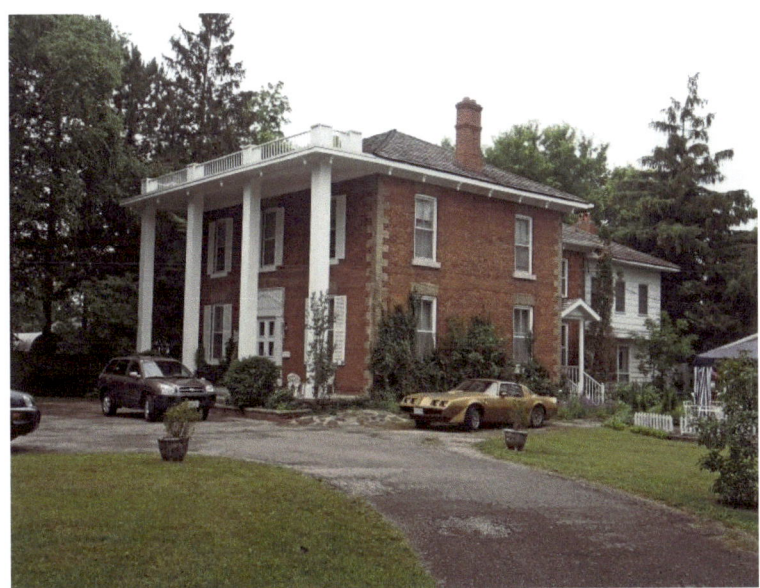

Struanhouse – R. Jacks – #329 – Victorian elegance in this historic brick home located on ¾ acre corner lot five blocks from downtown

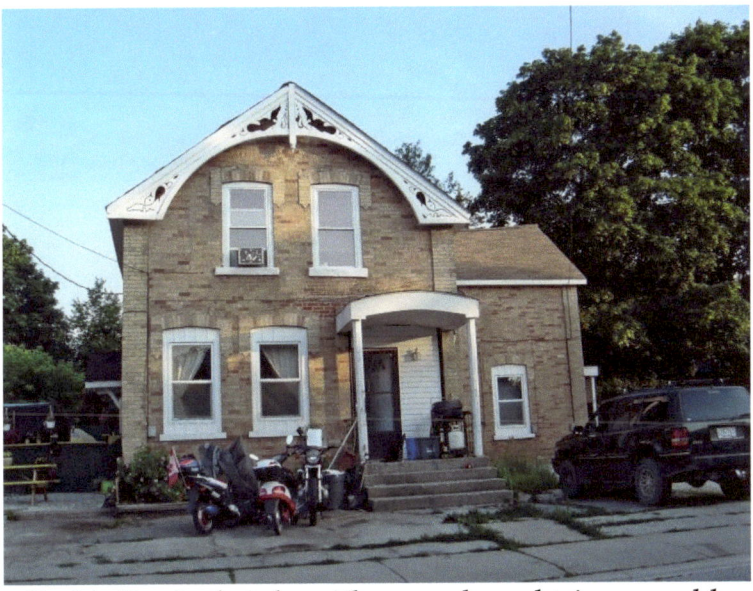

Gothic Revival style with verge board trim on gable

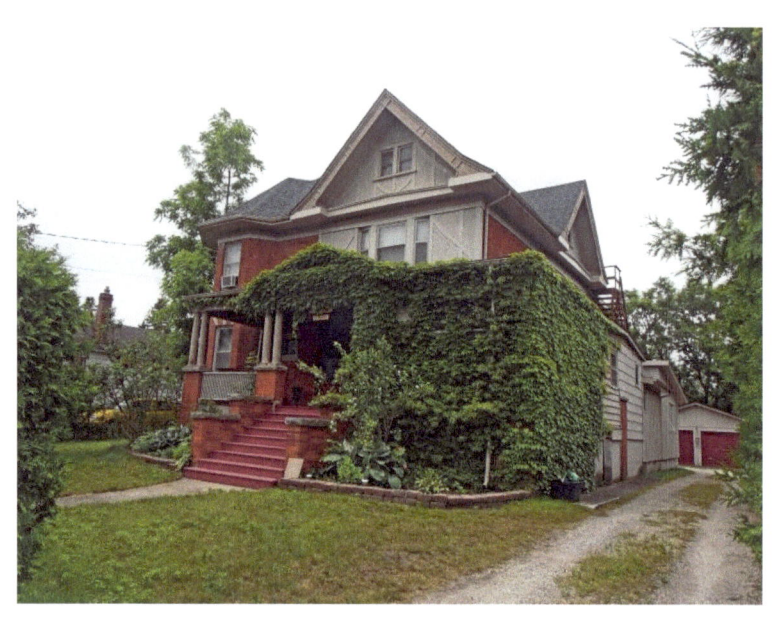

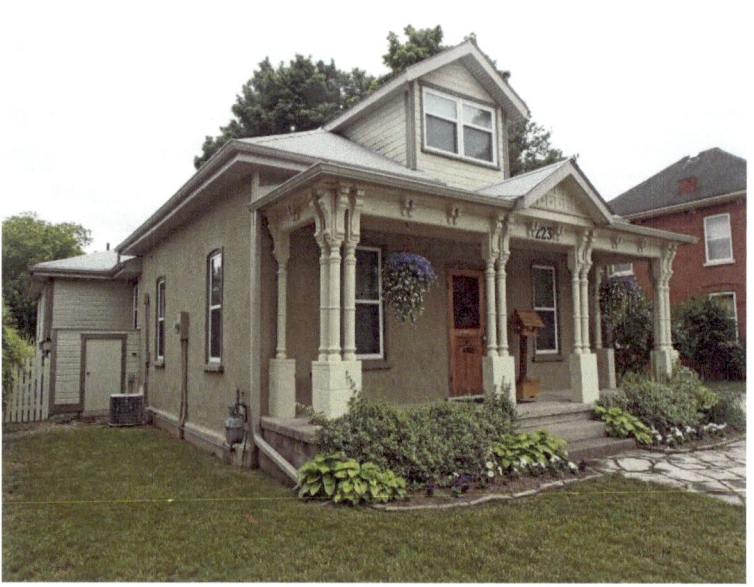

#223 – wood-turned verandah pillars

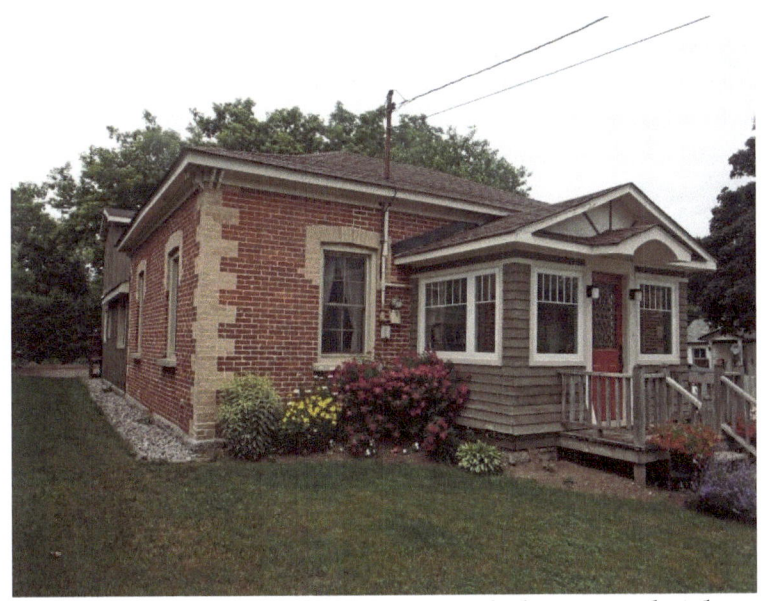

210 Cedar Street – Regency Cottage, dichromatic brickwork Hip roof

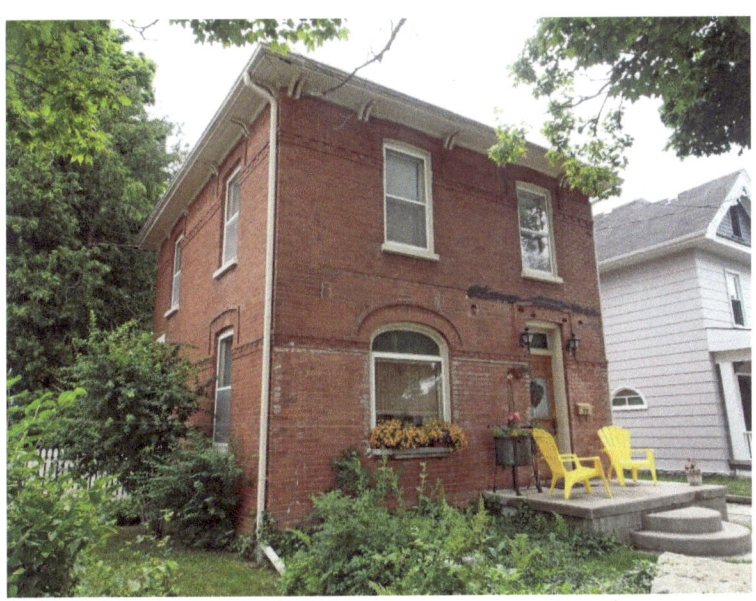

#233 – Italianate – paired cornice brackets

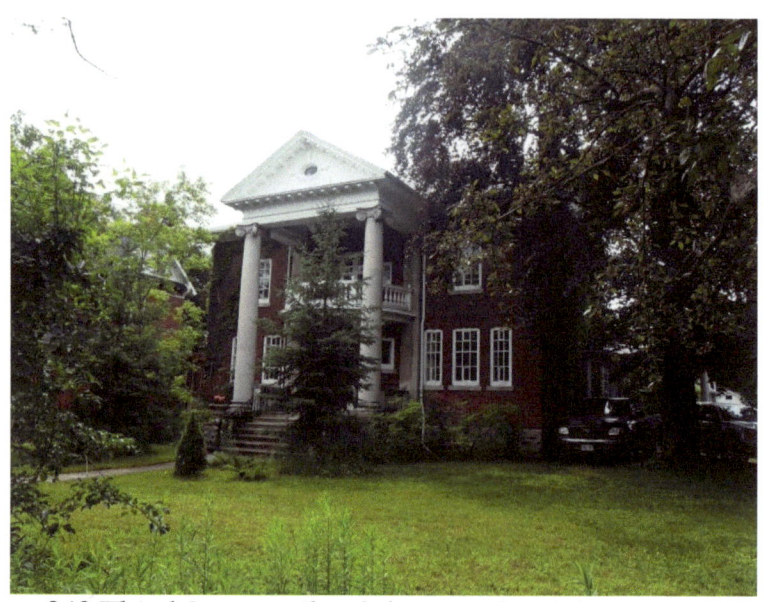

242 Third Street - This 2½ storey brick home was built for Charles Pitt, owner of the Bertram Lumber Company. John Wilson was the local Collingwood architect. The house was built in 1908 and is a Georgian influenced Neo-Classical home. A large pediment and column portico adorns the front façade. A balcony protrudes from the second floor within the pediment which has an elliptical window. Brick alternating radiating voussoirs adorn the window and door surround heads on the façade.

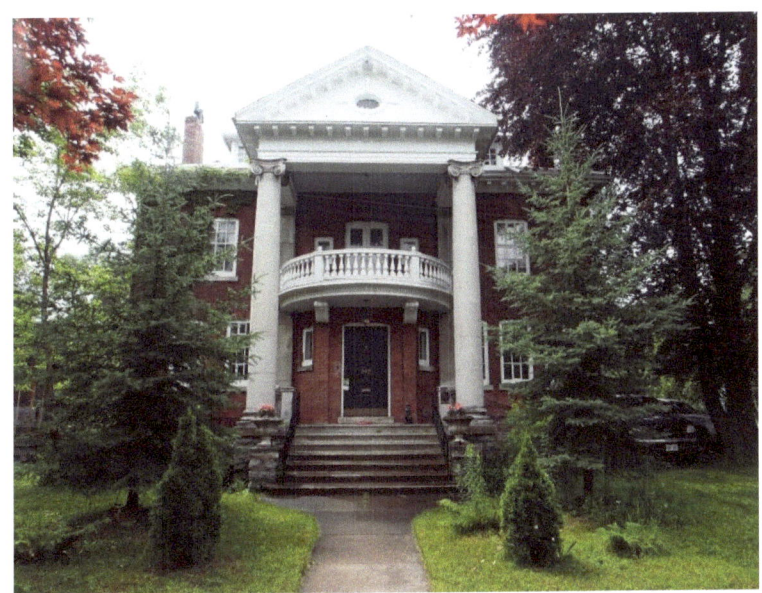

242 Third Street

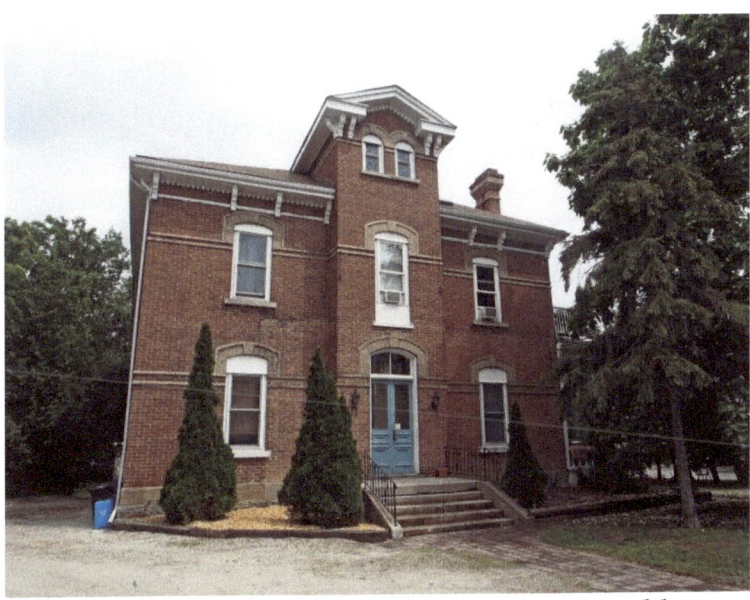

217 Third Street – Italianate – cornice return on gable, cornice brackets, 2½-storey frontispiece

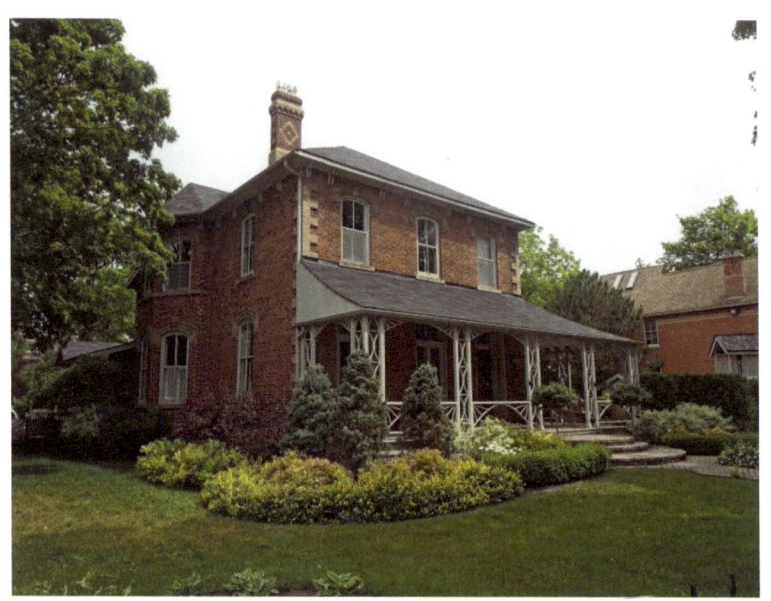

199 Third Street – Built in the Italianate tradition for the Toner family, early coal and lumber merchants, this home has retained its elegance with minor alterations since 1882. The interior of the home features a circular staircase, marble fireplaces, plaster medallions and a built in buffet.

The exterior brick work laid in the common bond tradition is highlighted by protruding quoins and plinth in lighter contrasting brick. Decorative brick work adorns the original chimney as well as highlighting the window openings. Brick arch work and keystones decorate the window surrounds in a unique three-tiered stepped arch design. The main front façade contains unique, French doors with recessed mullion and molded panels.

The home has a heavily bracketed low hip roof with an east side gable featuring a combination of corniced boxed brackets.

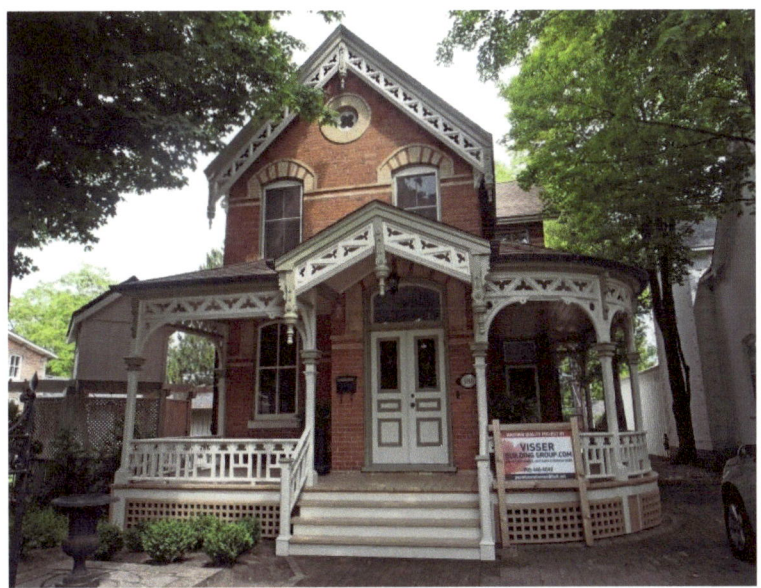

185 Third Street – elaborate verge board trim – Gothic Revival style – dichromatic brickwork banding and window voussoirs

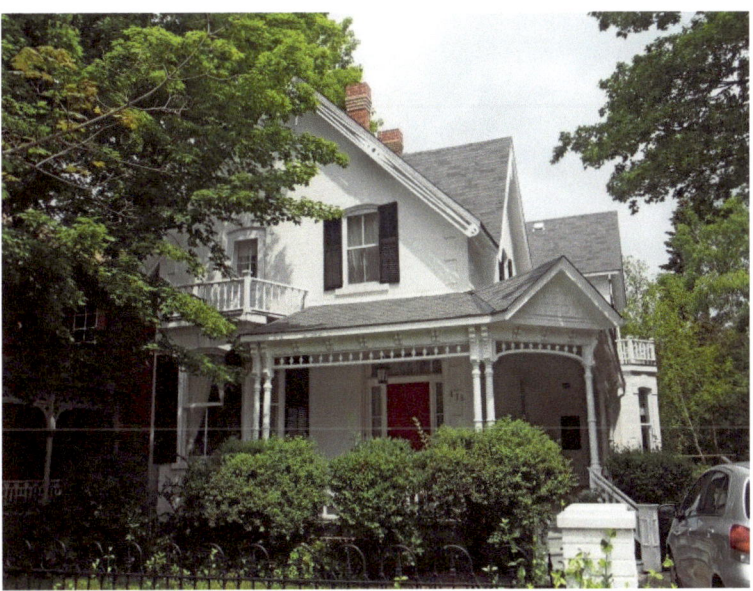

175 Third Street – Gothic Revival, second floor balcony

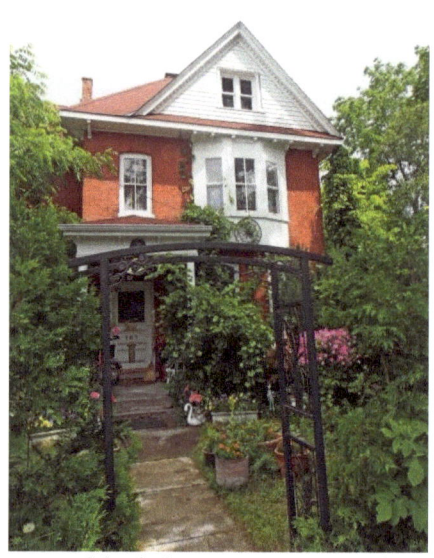

167 Third Street - gabled dormer in attic above bay window

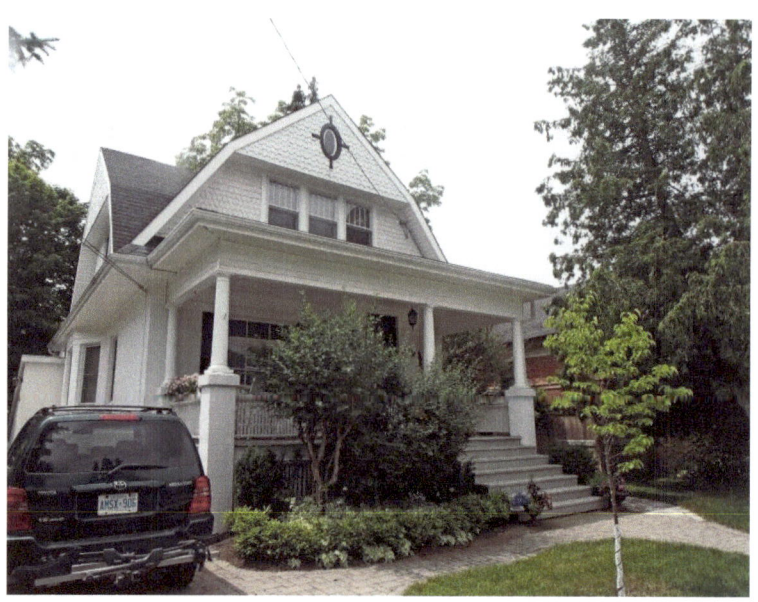

Neo-Colonial – gambrel roof

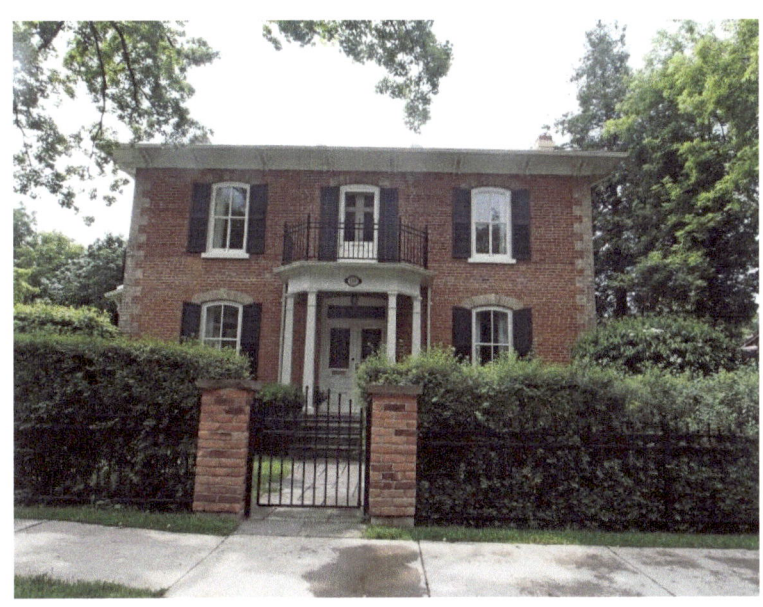

186 Third Street – Italianate style, balcony above entrance

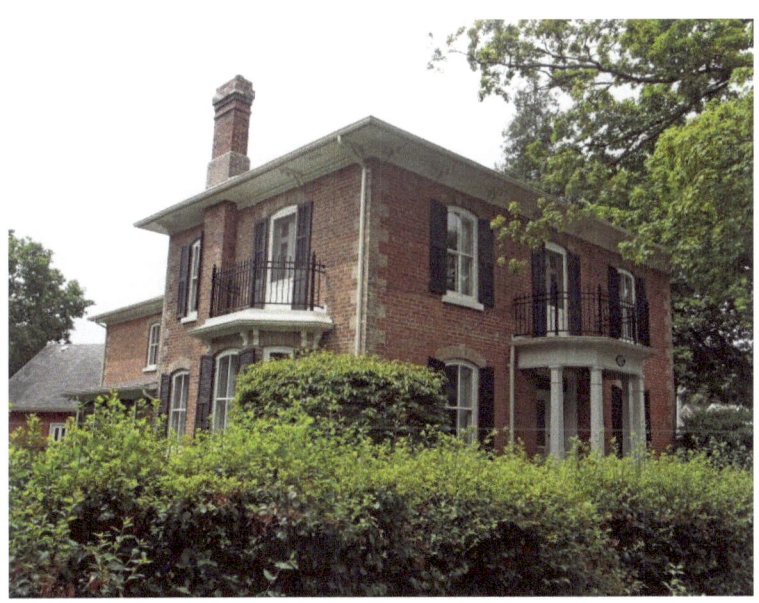

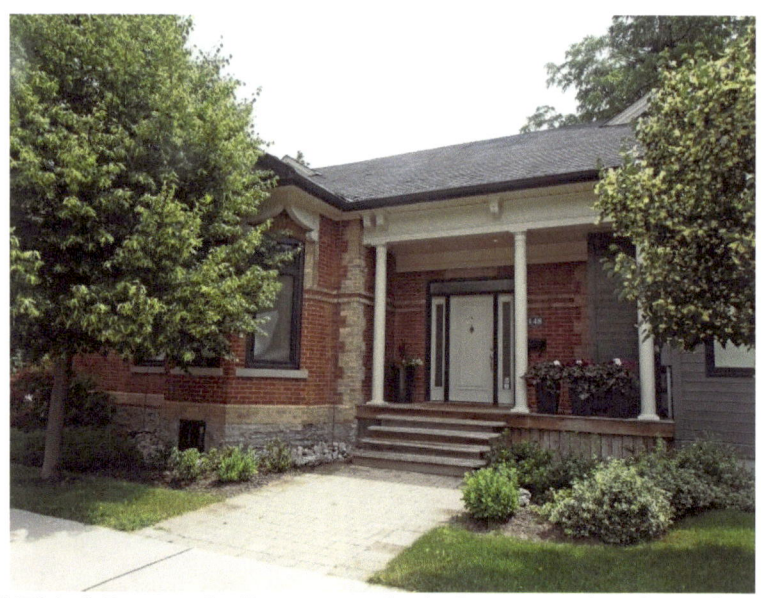

148 Third Street - Italianate with dichromatic brickwork, attic gable, quoining on corners, cornice brackets

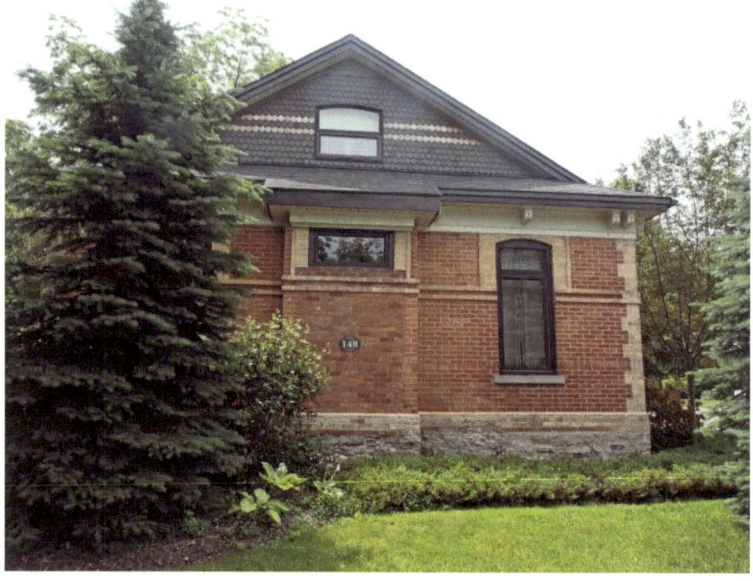

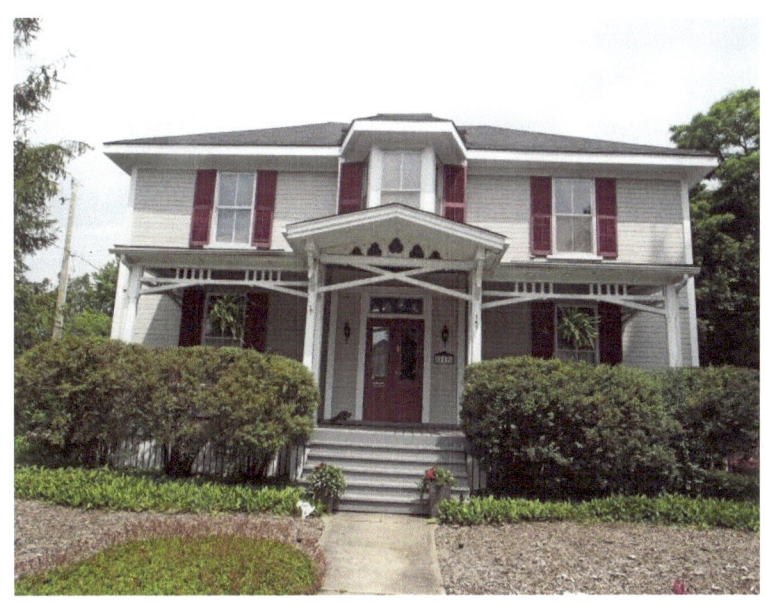

147 Third Street – Italianate with frontispiece
Upgraded with panelling

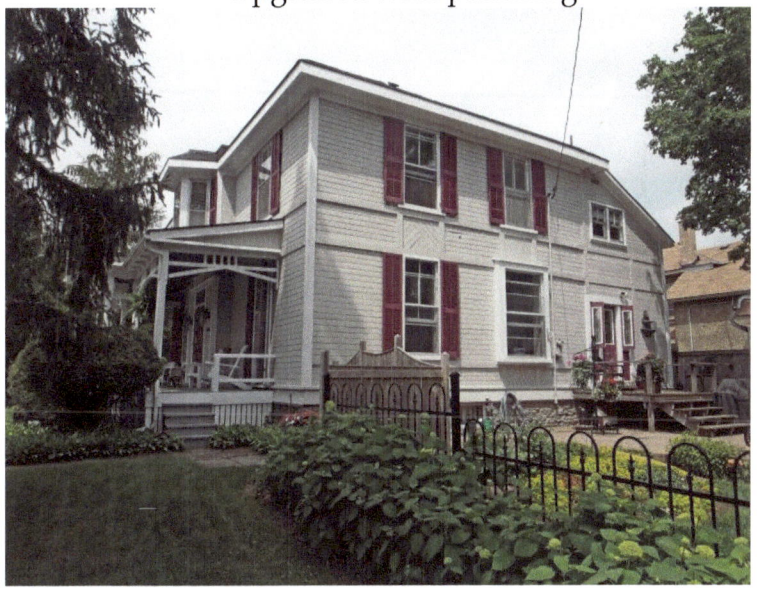

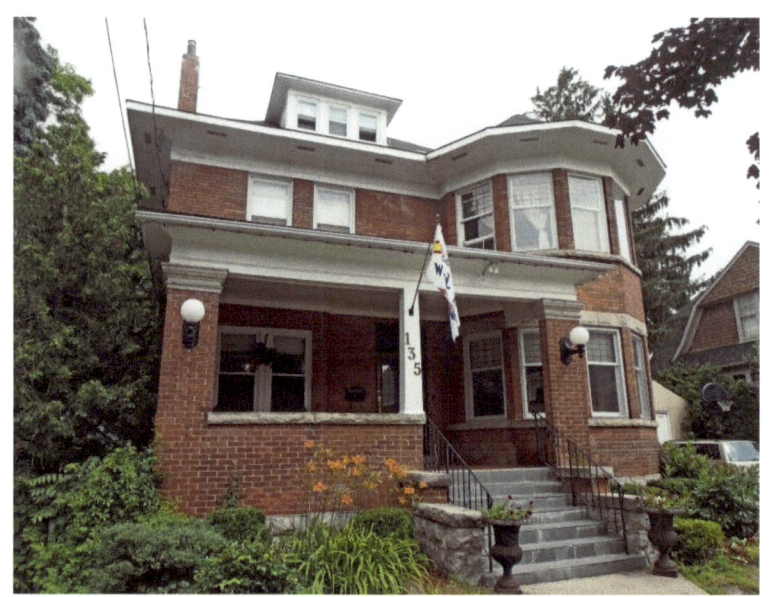

135 Third Street – two storey bay window, wide eaves, red brick, dormer out of roof

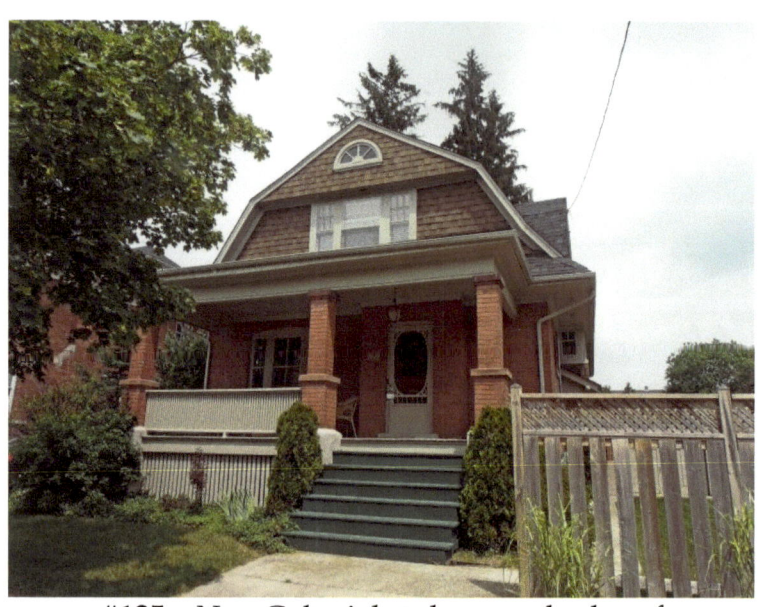

#125 – Neo-Colonial style – gambrel roof

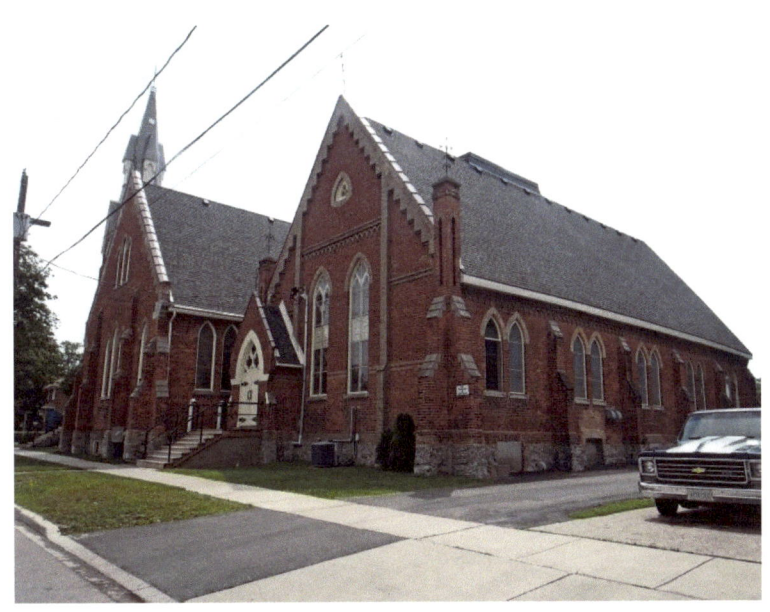

200 Maple Street – First Presbyterian Church, erected 1884
Red brick, buttresses

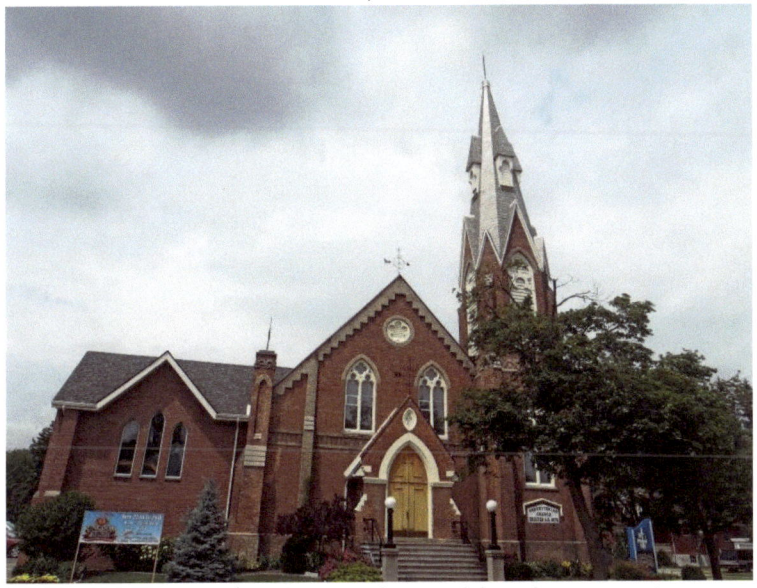

Lancet windows, lighter coloured brick voussoirs over windows

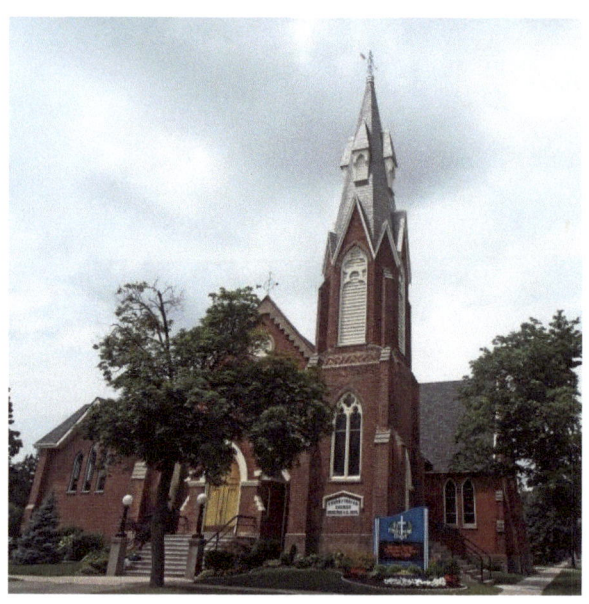

First Presbyterian Church – dichromatic brickwork

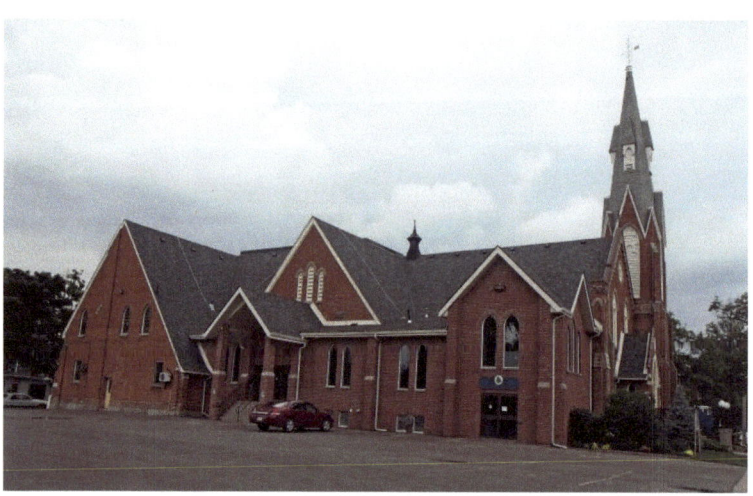

From rear

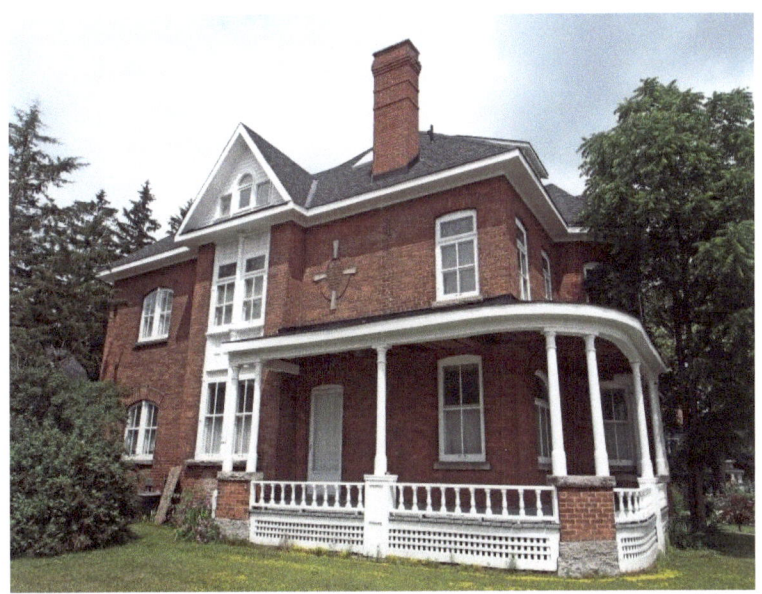

Italianate style with Palladian window in attic gable, wraparound veranda

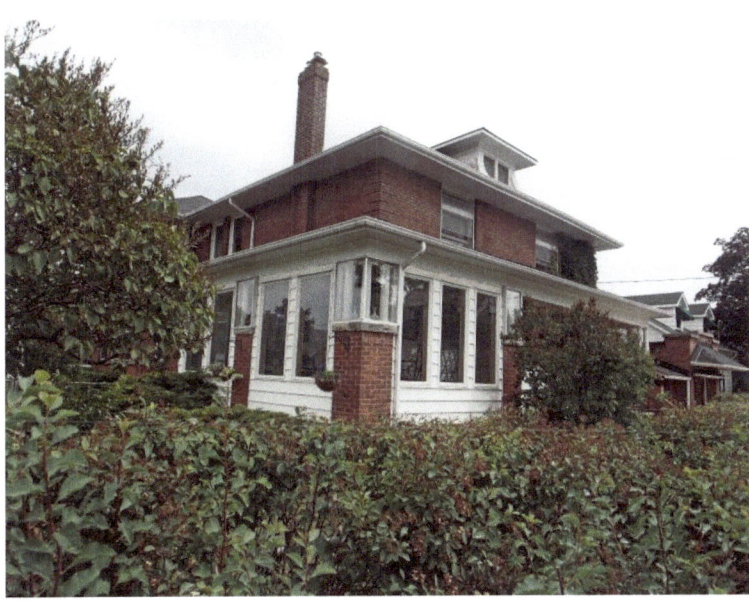

Dormer

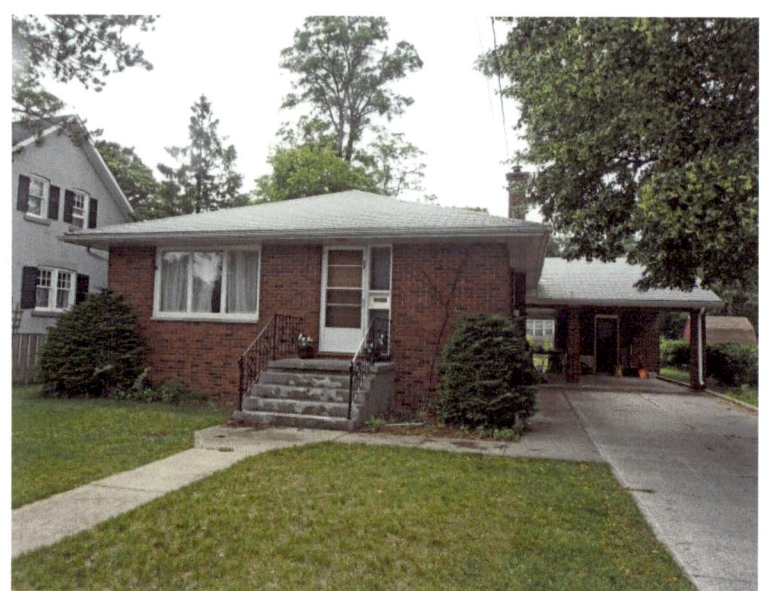
#88 - Regency Cottage, hipped roof

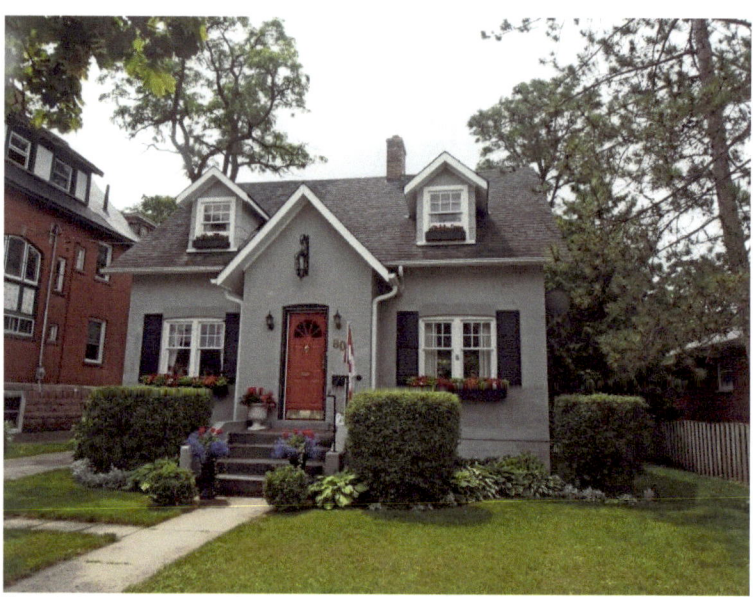
80 Third Street – Gothic Revival with dormer windows in attic

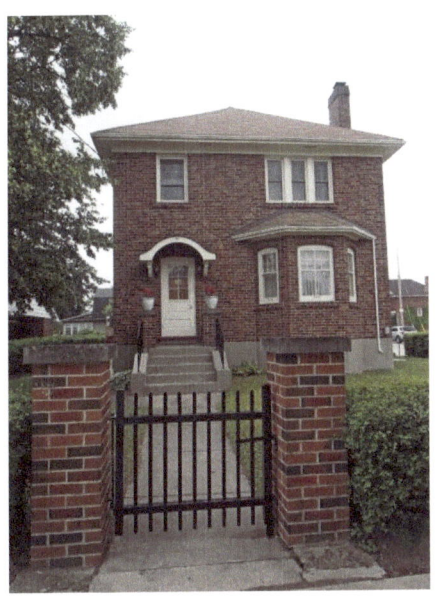

90 Third Street - Italianate with hipped roof, bay window, multi-coloured brick

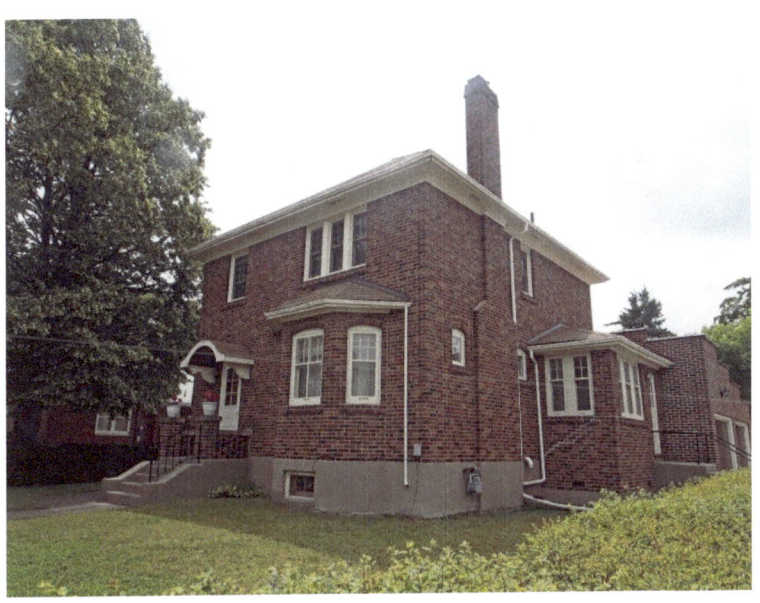

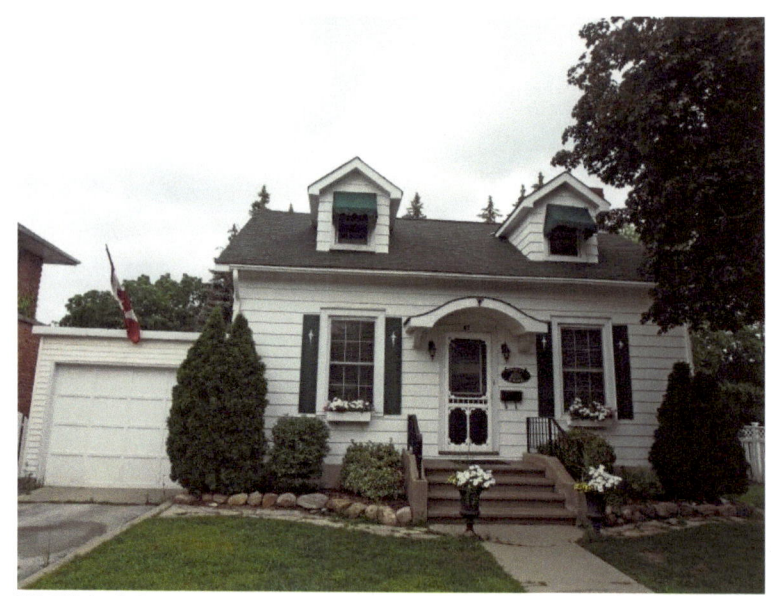

87 Third Street – Regency Cottage with dormers in attic

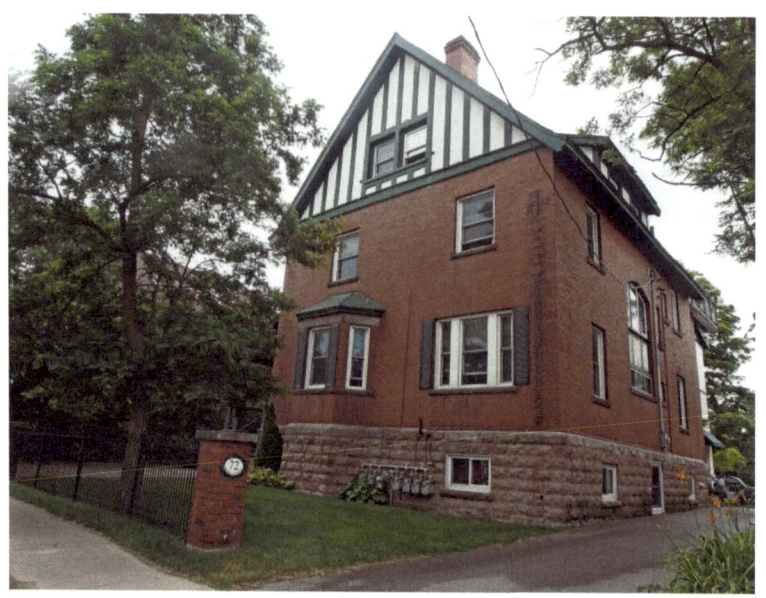

72 Third Street

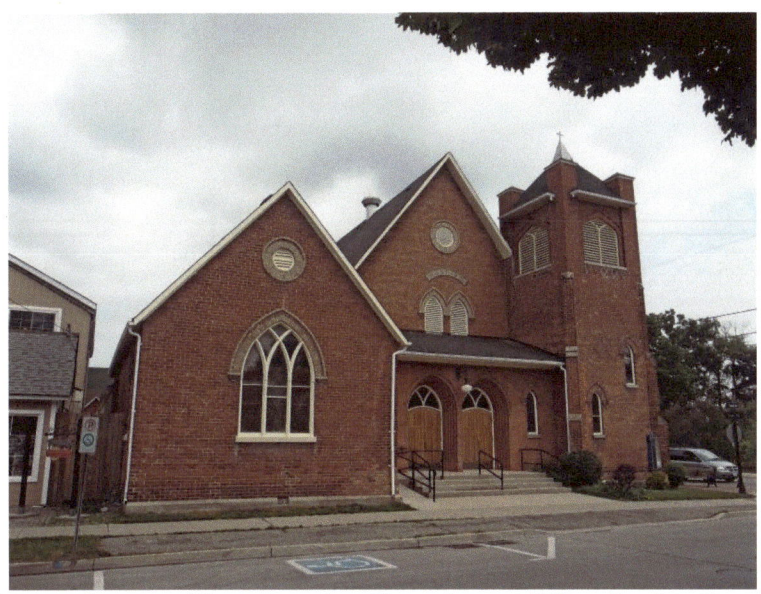

160 Pine Street - First Baptist Church, c. 1870s, Gothic Revival style

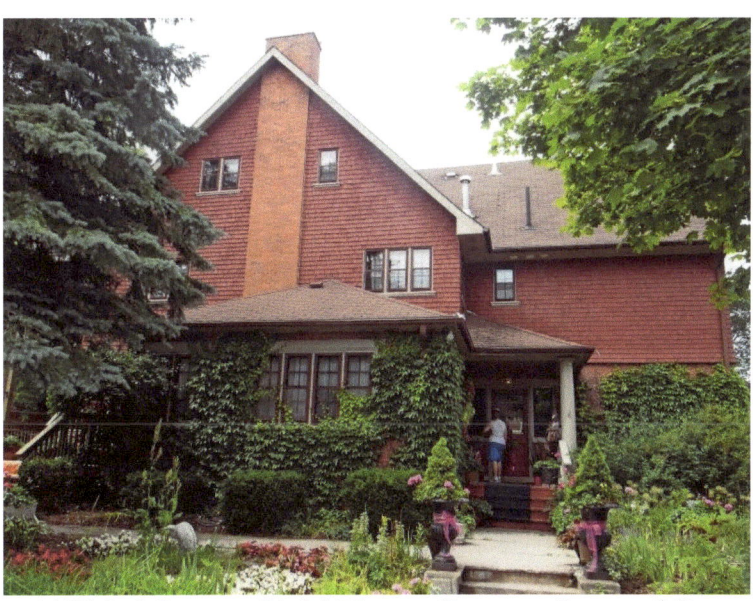

64 Third Street - Bield House Country Inn and Spa

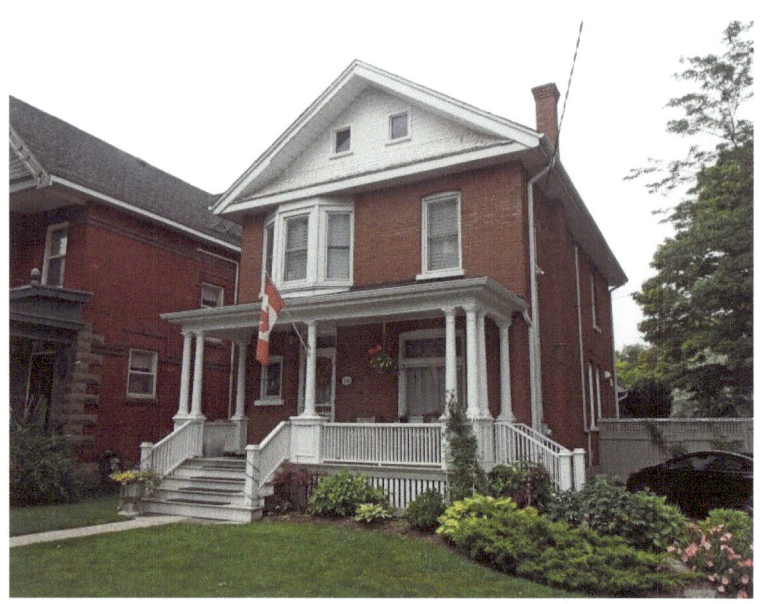

198 Pine Street - Edwardian style

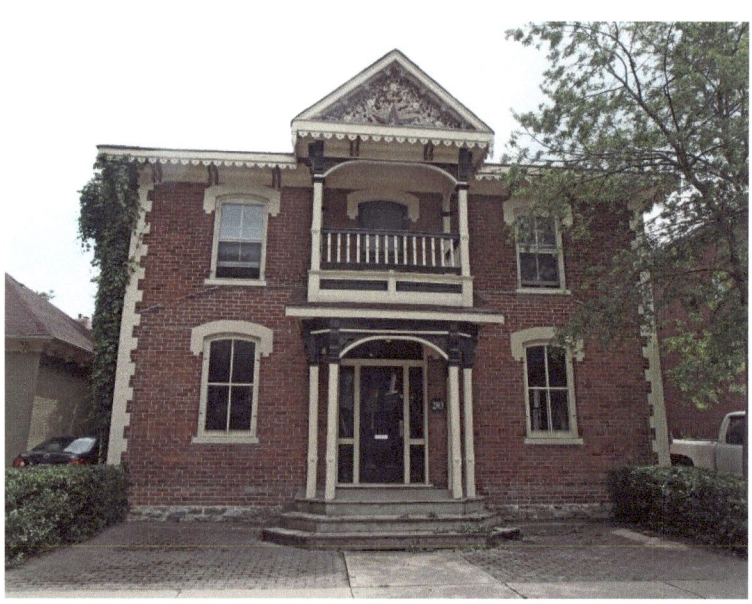

203 Pine Street – Italianate style – triangular pediment with decorated tympanum, lighter coloured window hoods, double cornice brackets, frontispiece supported by pillars

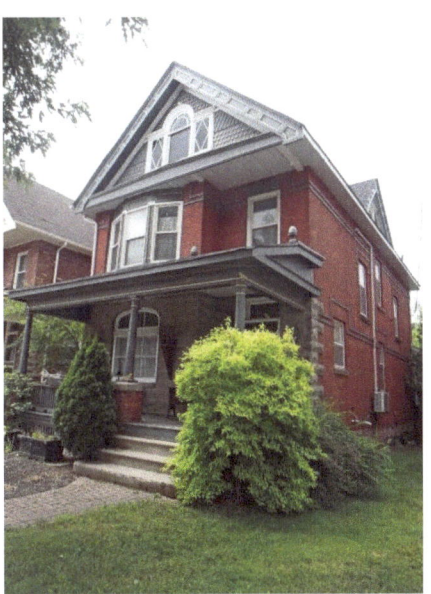

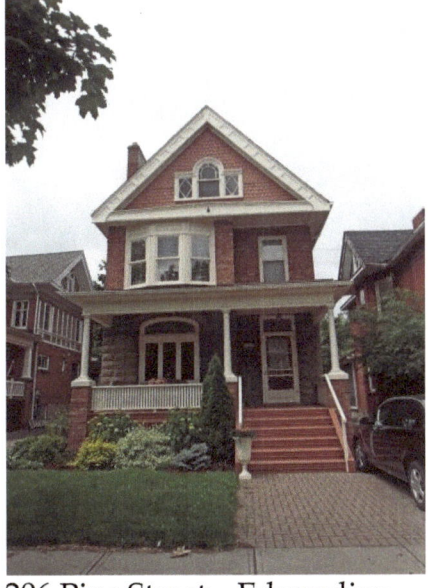

202 Pine Street – Edwardian style - quoining on corners, Palladian window in gable

206 Pine Street – Edwardian style – Palladian window, bay window on 2nd floor

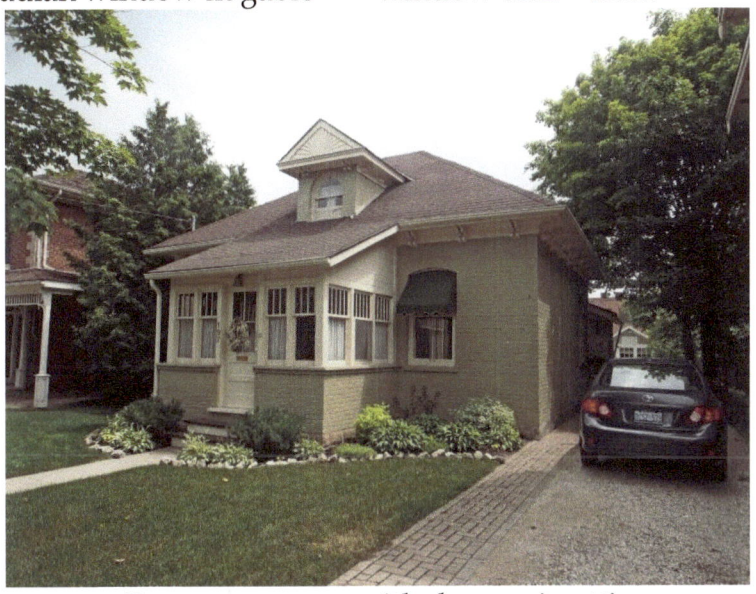

Regency cottage with dormer in attic

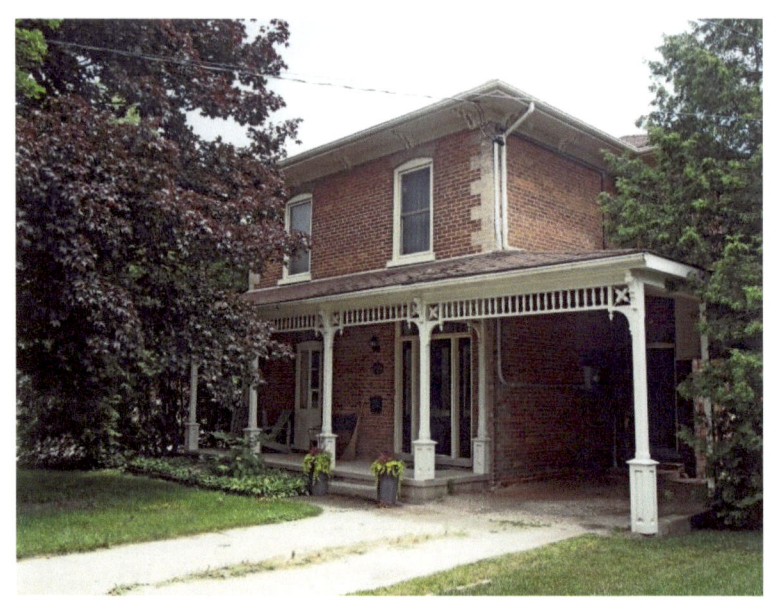

193 Pine Street – Italianate style

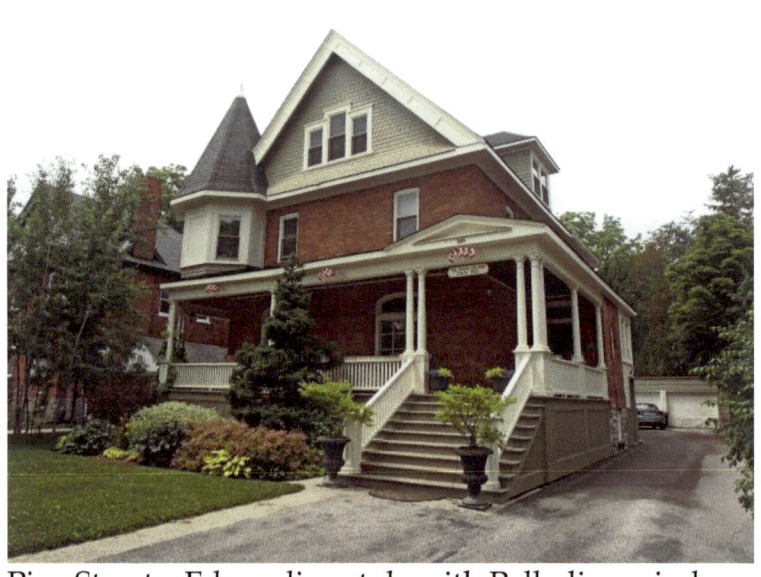

220 Pine Street – Edwardian style with Palladian window, and turret – c. 1910

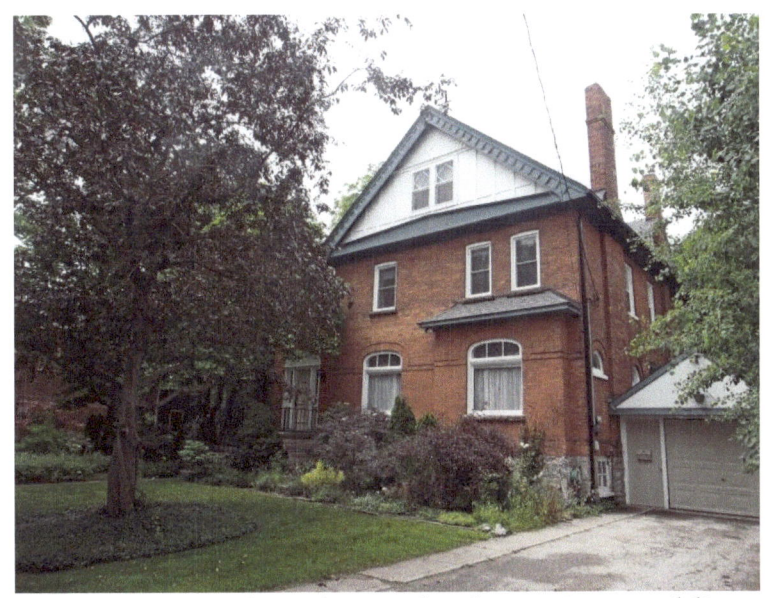

234 Pine Street – Edwardian style, decorative moulding on gable

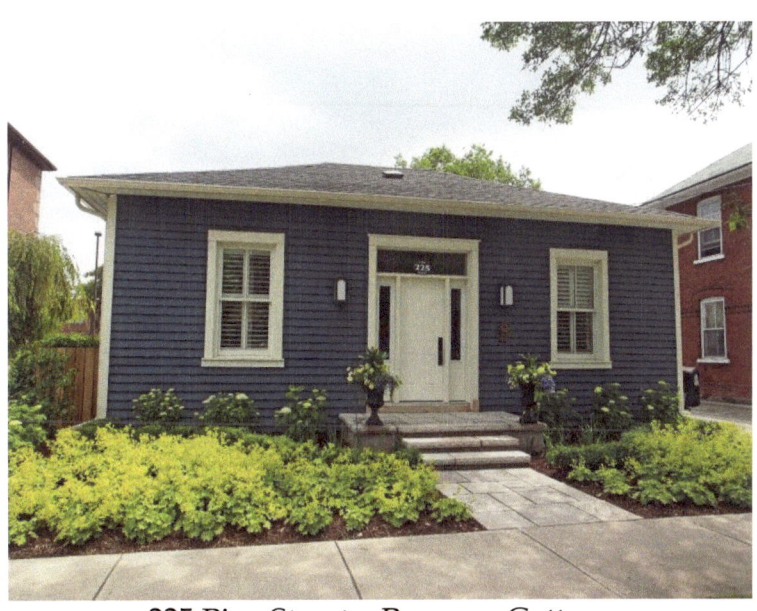

225 Pine Street – Regency Cottage

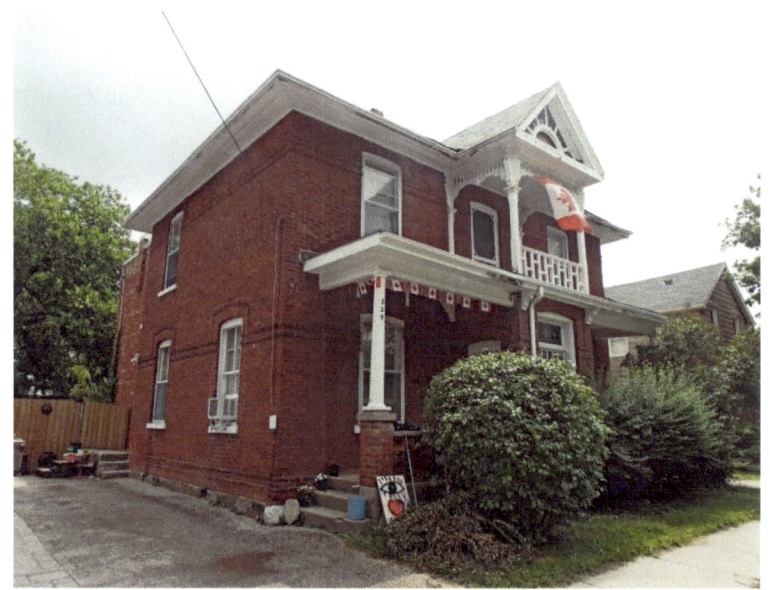

229 Pine Street - Italianate style with decorative frontispiece topped with triangular pediment and decorated tympanum

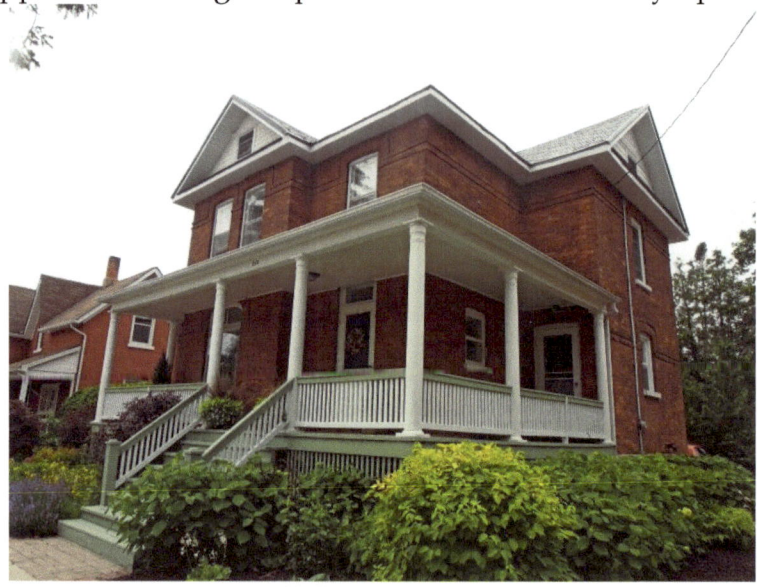

250 Pine Street

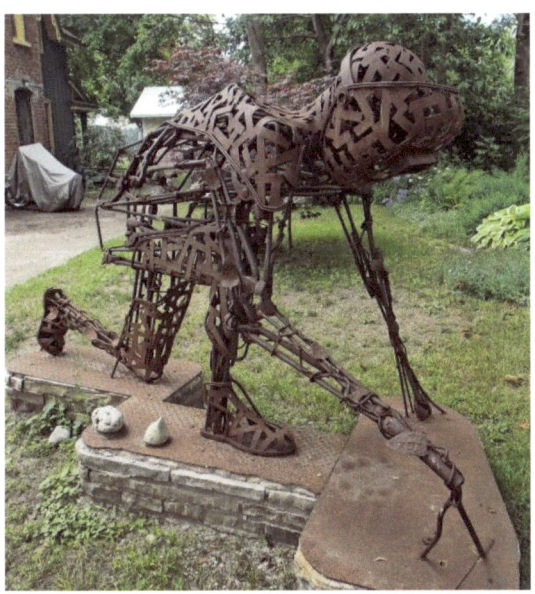

The Last Shift – John McCaffrey – 2009 – To honour and celebrate the many men and women of Collingwood who contributed their skills during a lifetime of work building ships at "The Yard" (1883-1986)

The Collingwood Shipyards 1883-1986

The sheltered harbor led wooden side-wheelers to call at this port, originally known as Hen and Chickens Harbour. When the railway arrived in 1855, steamers picked up passengers and freight bound for destinations all around the lakes. The level of shipping out of the port, now known as Collingwood, increased so much that the need for dry dock services was clear. Local mariners and businessmen succeeded in opening The Queen's Dry Dock on May 24, 1883, named in honor of Queen Victoria's birthday. Over the 103 year history of shipbuilding in this community, the company had many names and changes in ownership. Locally it will always be known as The Collingwood Shipyard.

From this site, the lakes finest and often biggest wooden passenger vessels were side-launched into Georgian Bay. The Majestic and Germanic were two of many wooden vessels launched here before the turn of the century. Construction methods changed to steel in 1900. The workers worked as blacksmiths, burners, carpenters, chippers, crane operators, drafters, drillers, joiners, laborers, machinists, management, painters, platers, plumbers, riggers, riveters, shipwrights, stagers, storekeepers, tinsmiths and truck drivers. The Yard was at the heart of the community. There was a sound to shipbuilding: riveters banging against the hull, alarms of the cranes in motion along the crane tracks, the whistle signaling the beginning and end of a shift, lunch hour and coffee break. Before the advent of radar, operators of small craft found the harbor by the spark and sound of the welders' torches.

Ships were constructed in sections and assembled on the launchways, beside the slip where they would be launched. Piece by piece, freighters, ferries, corvettes and trawlers took shape at the end of Hurontario Street. The constant present of the "ship at the end of the street" reminded residents and visitors that Collingwood built ships and did so with pride. More than 200 steel ships were built by Collingwood men and women. The exact number of wooden vessels built from 1883 to 1900 is unknown.

Launching a Ship

There were always thousands of people on hand watching when Collingwood Shipyards launched a new hull using the side launch method. Hulls were built almost two meters above ground level and blocked up by huge wooden timbers.

When the hull was ready to launch, forty-seven launch ways were placed under the hull at an angle sloping down toward the launch basin. Well-greased butter boards were placed on the ways to ease the passage of the hull. Trigger assemblies were placed along the length of the ship and over two hundred men with sledgehammers hammered wedges under the ship until it was lifted off its block and on the launch ways, held back by steel cleats at the end of the butter boards and the triggers. Under the directions of the launch master, the steel cleats were removed, the men cleared from beneath the ship, and axe men took up their stations beside the trigger ropes holding the ship back. At a signal, the ropes were cut simultaneously and the ship would slide down into the launch basin displacing a huge wall of water as it went.

When the Yard closed in 1986, the Collingwood Shipyard was the only company in Canada which still used the side launch method of getting hulls into the water.

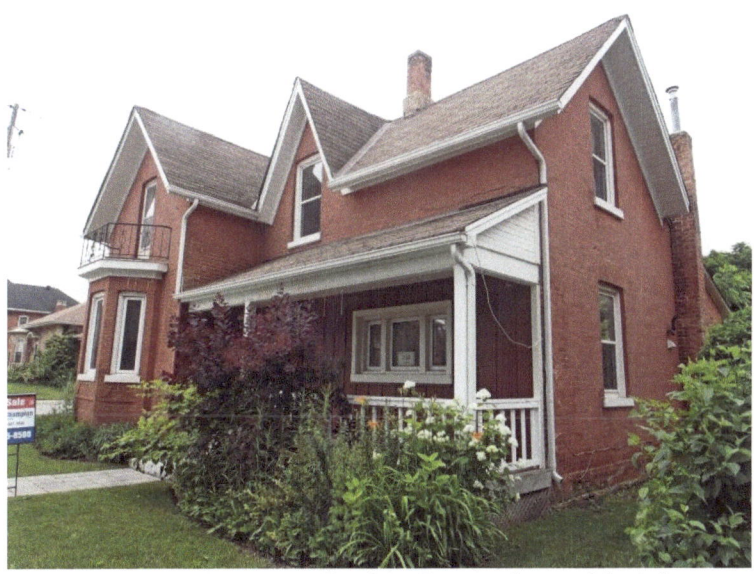

258 Pine Street – Gothic Revival – red brick

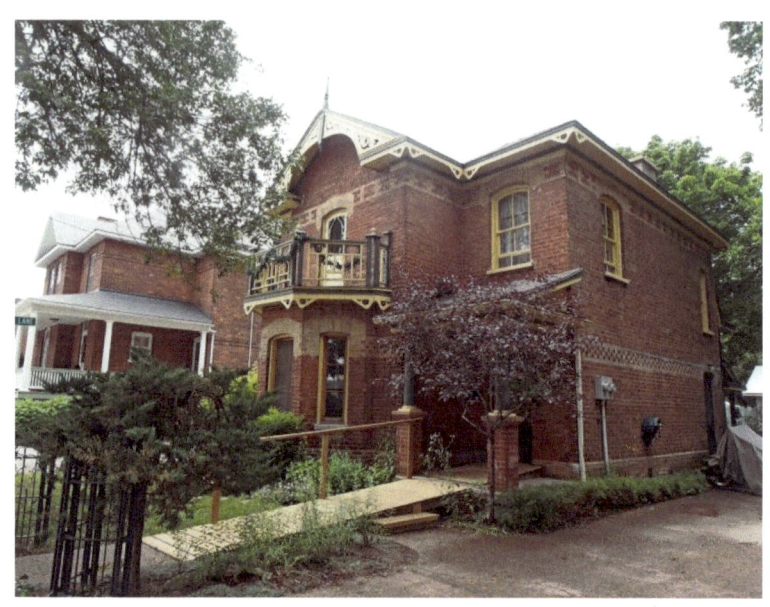

242 Pine Street - Italianate with Gothic style frontispiece, verge board and finial, dichromatic brickwork

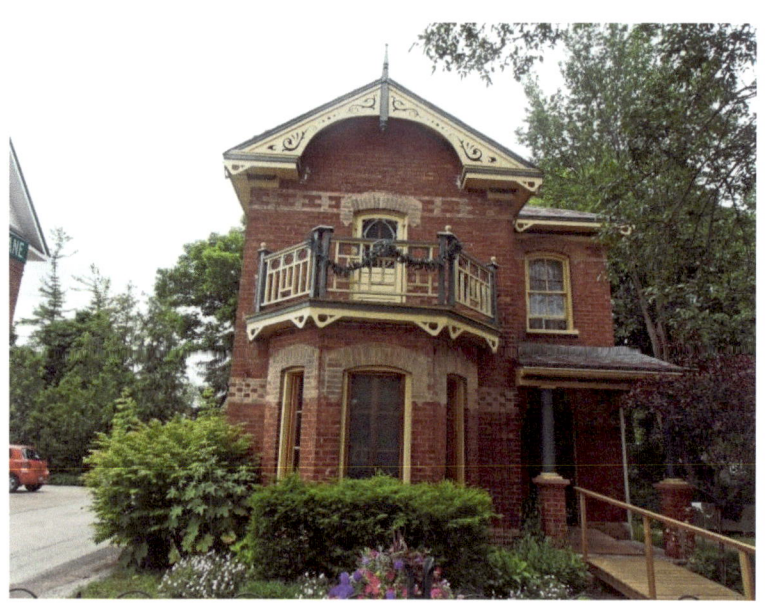

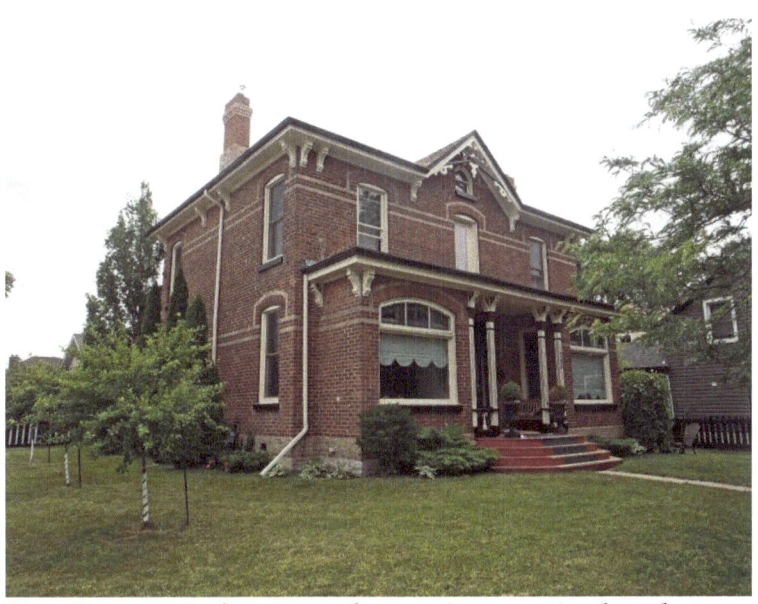

265 Pine Street – Italianate – decorative cornice brackets, verge board trim on small gable, dichromatic brickwork

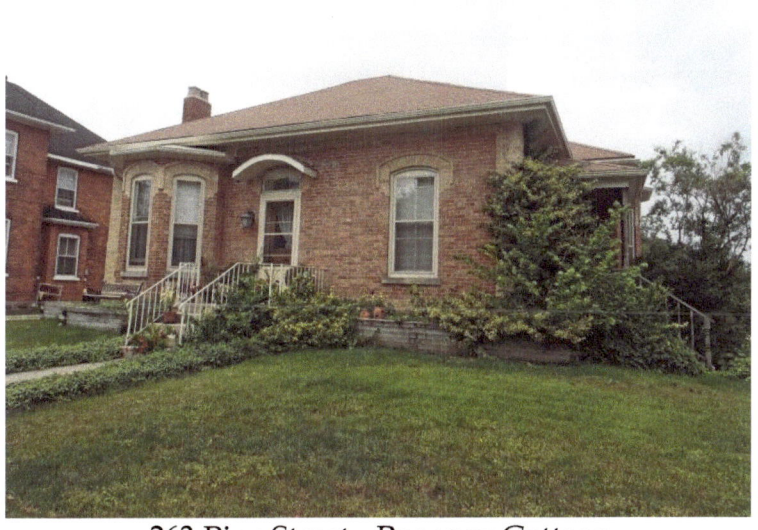

263 Pine Street - Regency Cottage

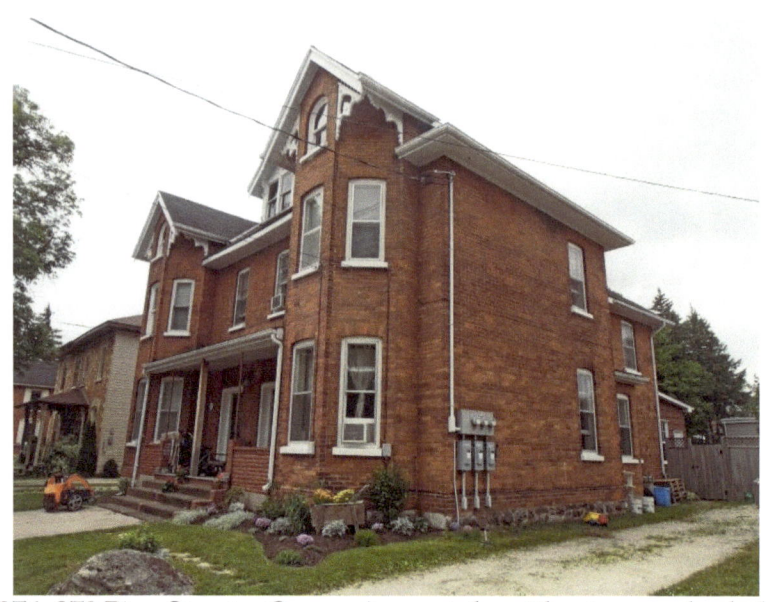

276, 278 Pine Street – Queen Anne style with a two-and-a-half storey tower-like bay with projecting eaves and large fretwork pieces resembling brackets; stone basement wall

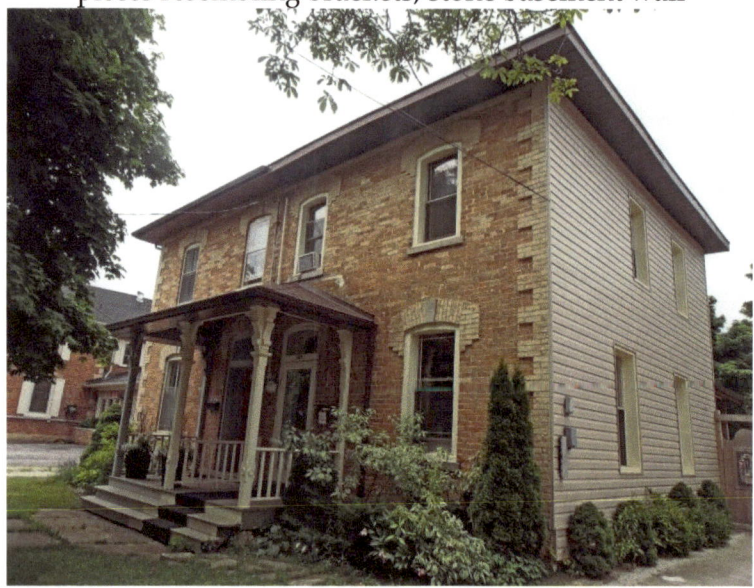

284, 286 Pine Street – Italianate style yellow-orange brick, quoin on corners, voussoirs above windows in buff coloured brick

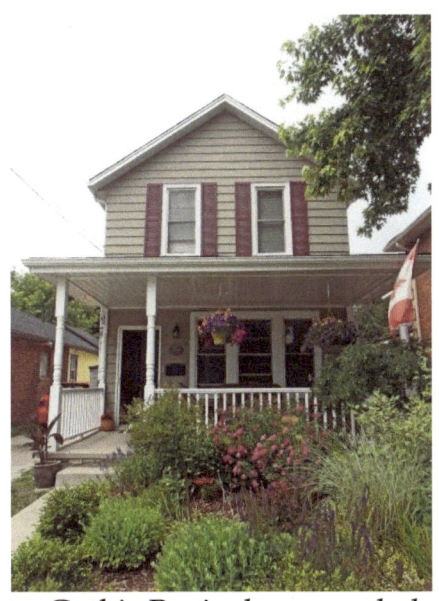

300 Pine Street – Gothic Revival – upgraded with panelling

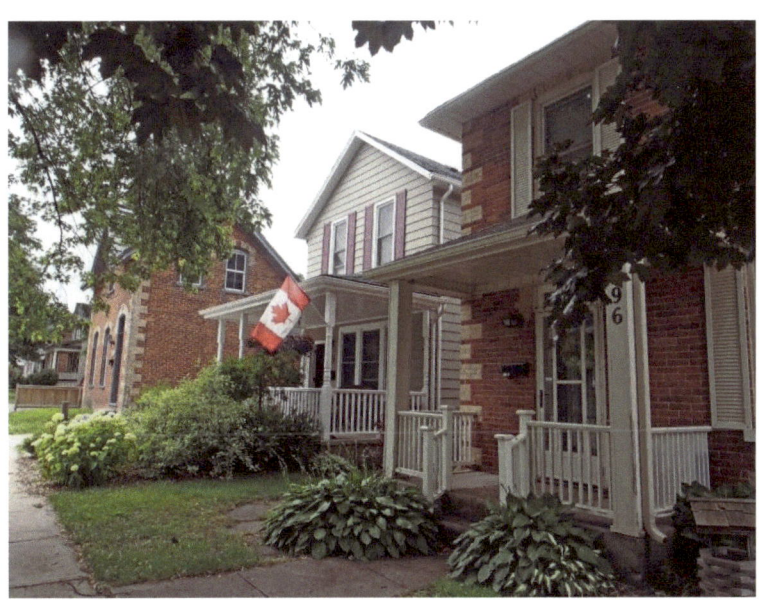

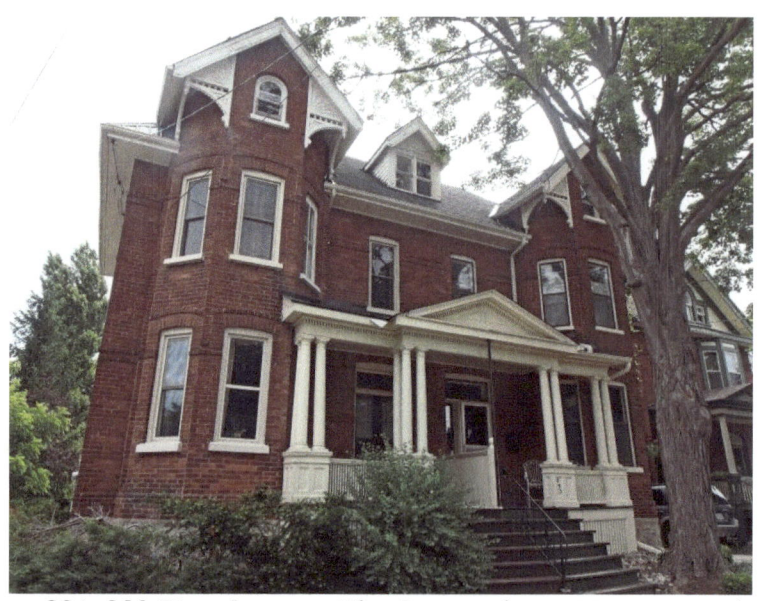

291, 293 Pine Street – The Stoutenburg House was built in 1904 with elements of the fanciful Queen Anne Revival style. With its twin stacked bay windows, center roof gable and formal porch spanning both front entries, the building is large. It is a semi-detached dwelling which local sawmill owner Peter Stoutenburg had constructed with a view to providing a home for two of his many daughters.

The Classical open porch with its triple column clusters, the stacked bay window with decorated gables with large fretwork pieces resembling brackets, the door case, and center roof dormer incorporate some of the more stylish manufactured building components available at that date.

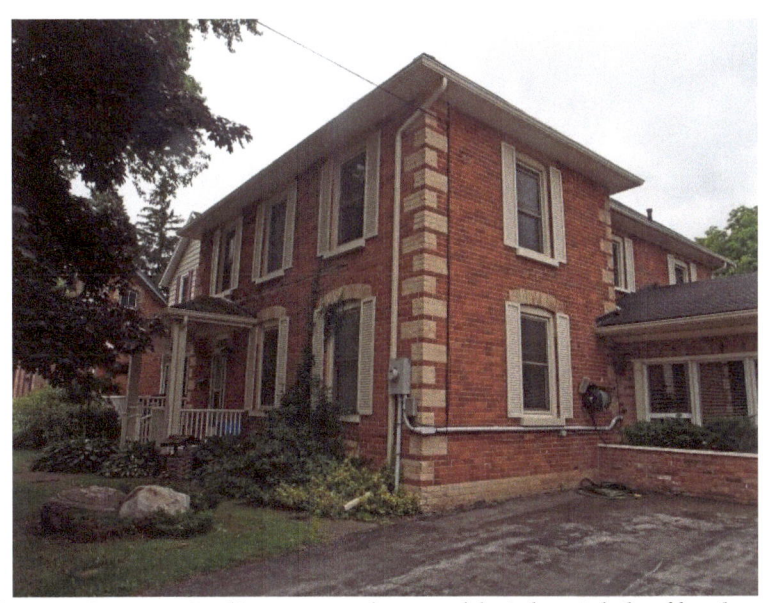

296 Pine Street – Italianate style – red brick with buff coloured accents

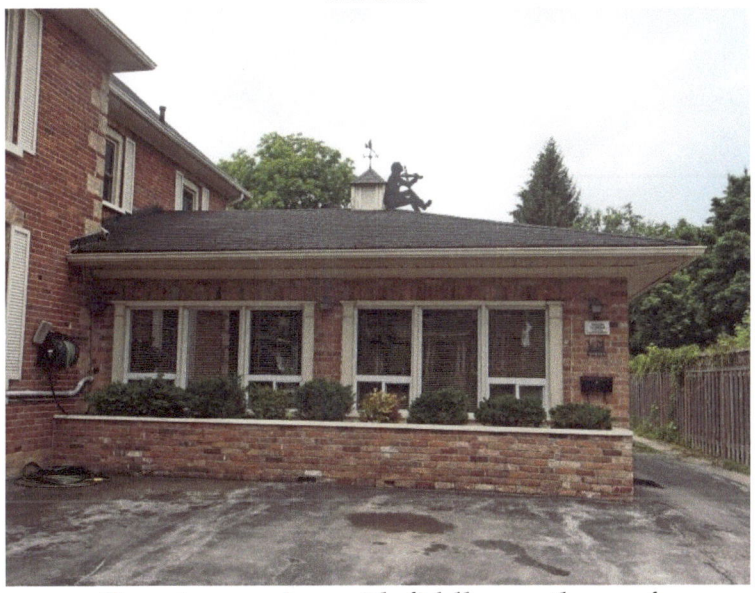

One storey wing with fiddler on the roof
The first date Harry and I went on was to see
"Fiddler on the Roof"

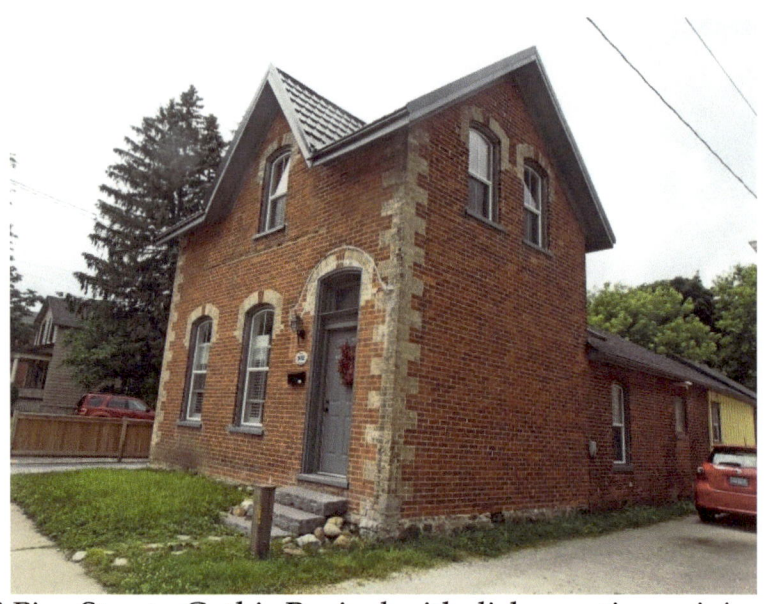

302 Pine Street - Gothic Revival with dichromatic quoining on corners, and buff coloured voussoirs

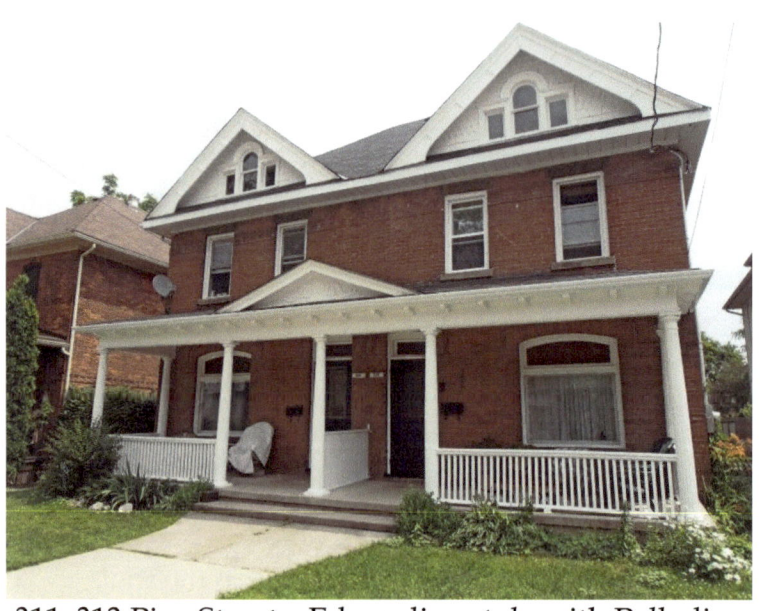

311, 313 Pine Street – Edwardian style with Palladian windows in gables

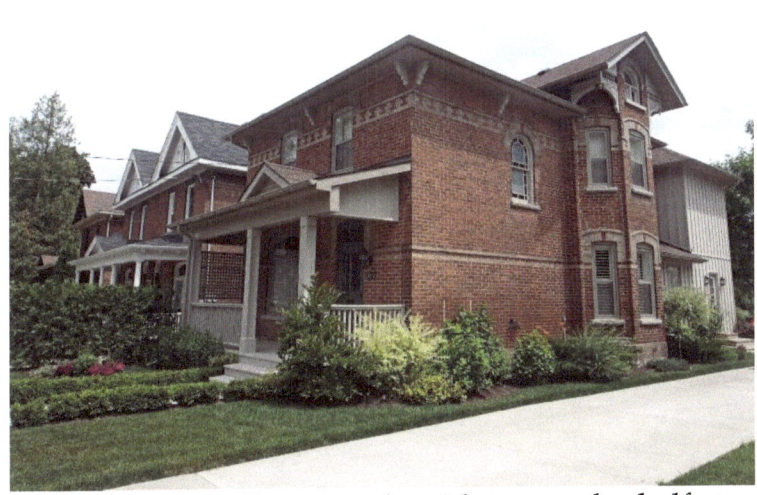

317 Pine Street - Italianate style with two-and-a-half-storey bay with projecting eaves and large fretwork pieces resembling brackets.

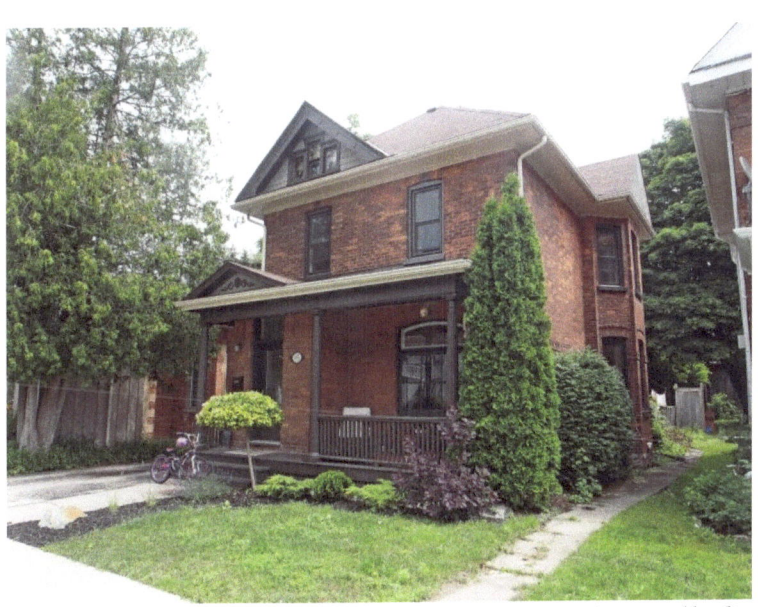

305 Maple Street – Edwardian/Italianate style – Palladian window, triangular pediment with decorated tympanum

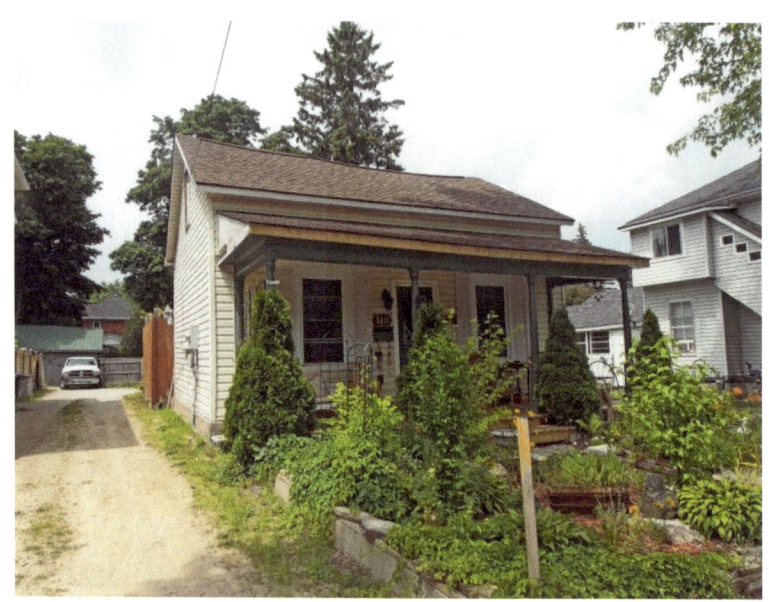
310 Pine Street

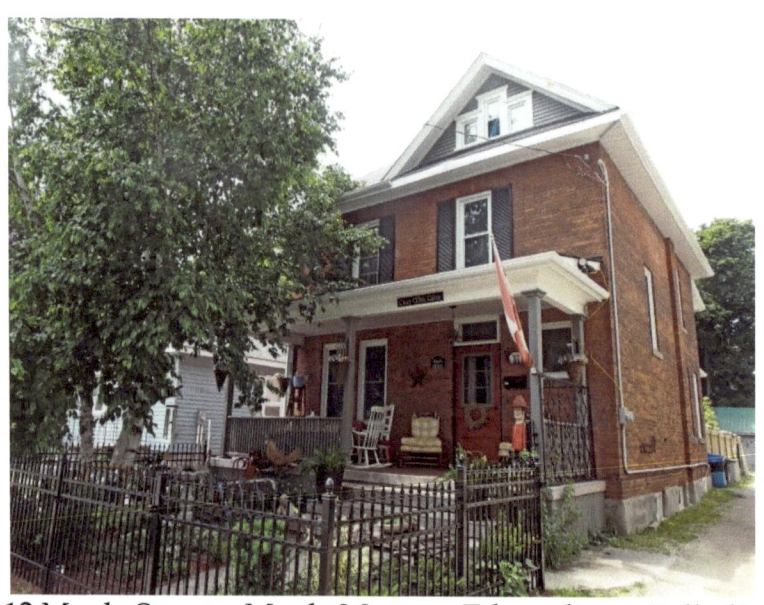
312 Maple Street – Maple Manor – Edwardian – Palladian window

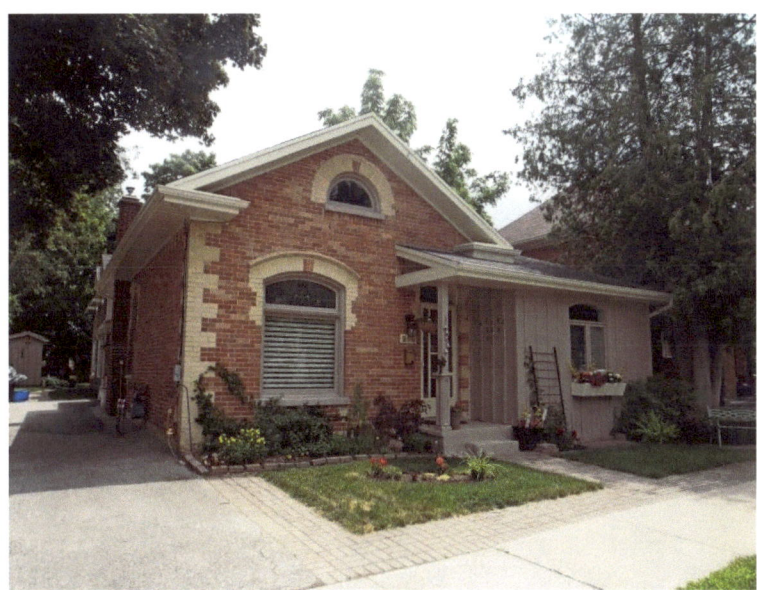

299 Maple Street – 1½ storey Gothic cottage with dichromatic brickwork, buff coloured voussoirs, keystones colour of walls, and cornice return on gable

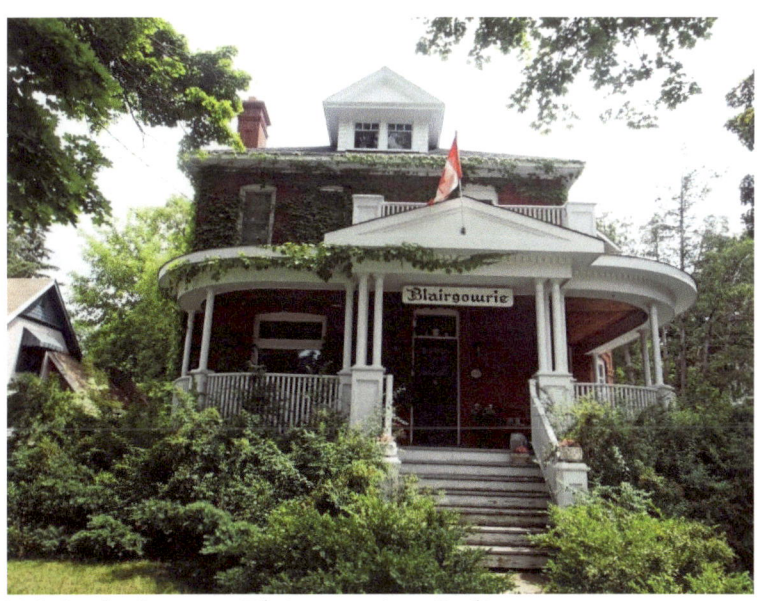

291 Maple Street – Blairgowrie – Italianate – wrap-around verandah, triangular pediment supported by pillars

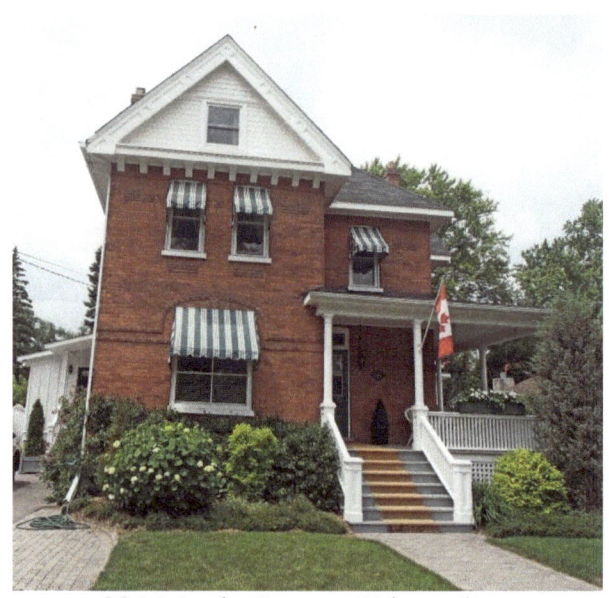

284 Maple Street – Edwardian

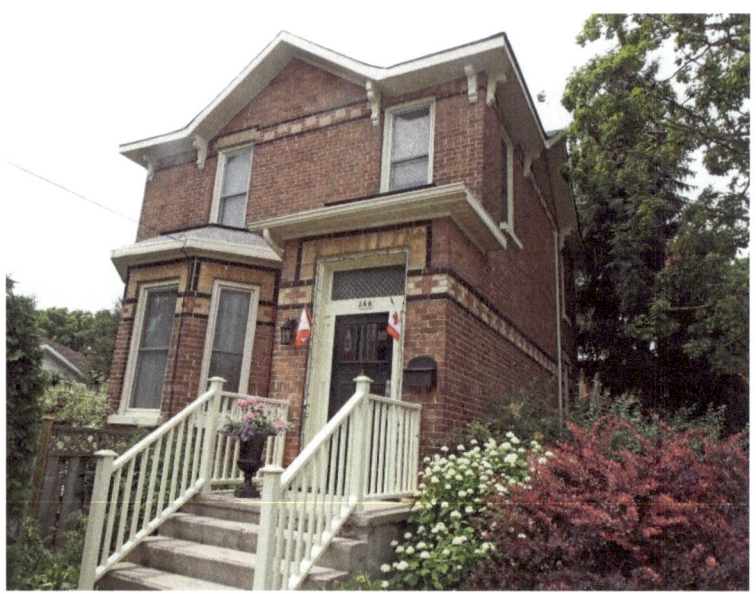

266 Maple Street - Italianate – dichromatic decorative brickwork, bay window, single cornice brackets

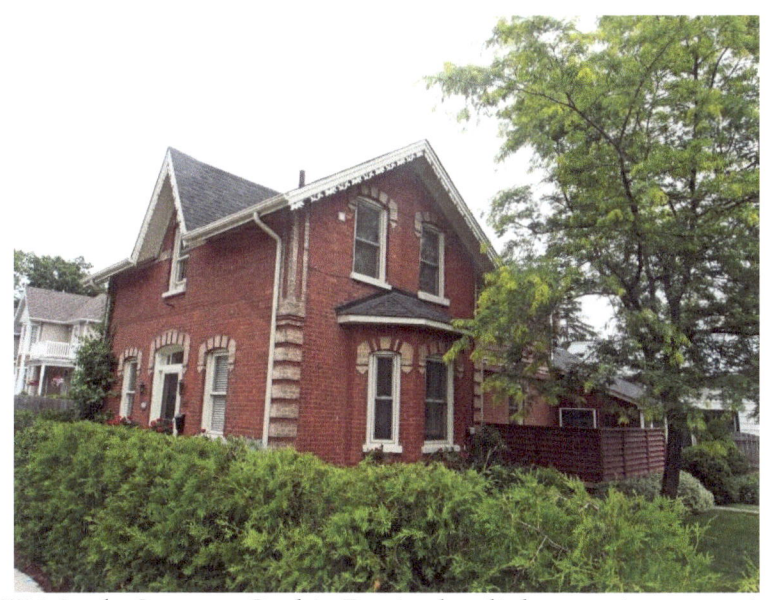

255 Maple Street – Gothic Revival – dichromatic voussoirs, verge board on gables, corner quoins

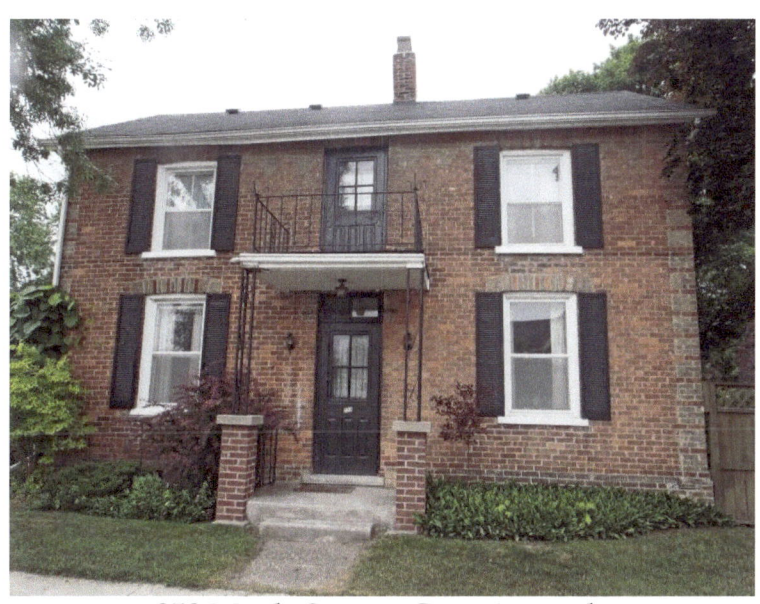

258 Maple Street - Georgian style

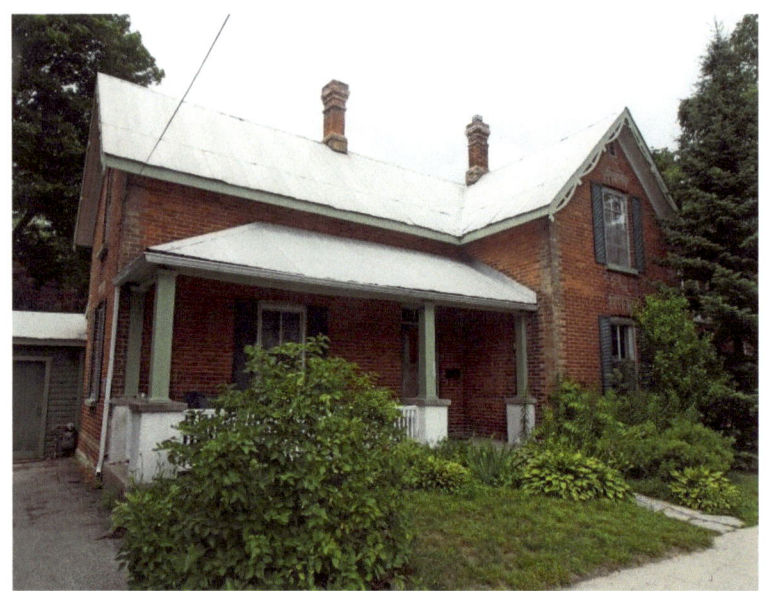

250 Maple Street – Gothic Revival, verge board trim on gable

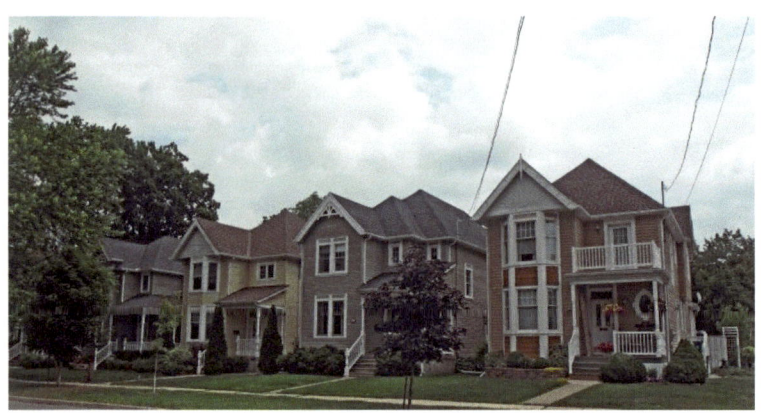

Gothic Revival – upgraded with siding – verge board and finial on gables

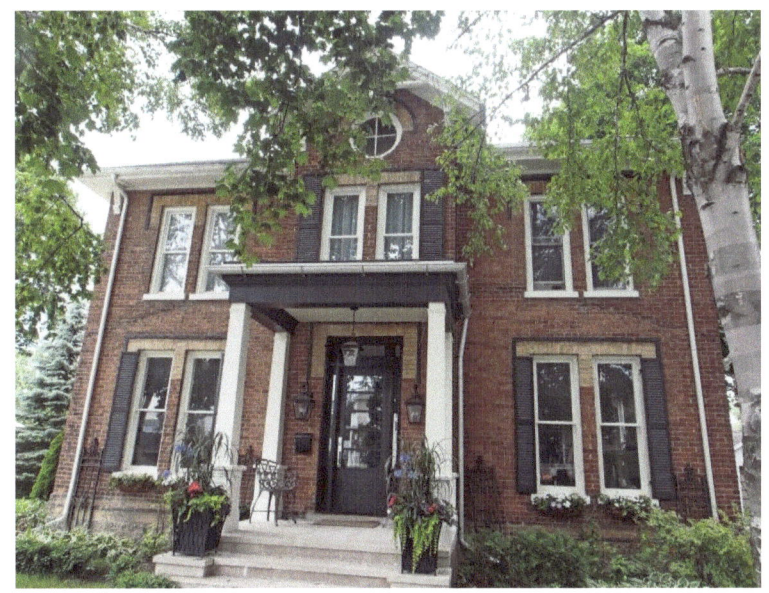

Italianate style, frontispiece with square pillars, decorated gable

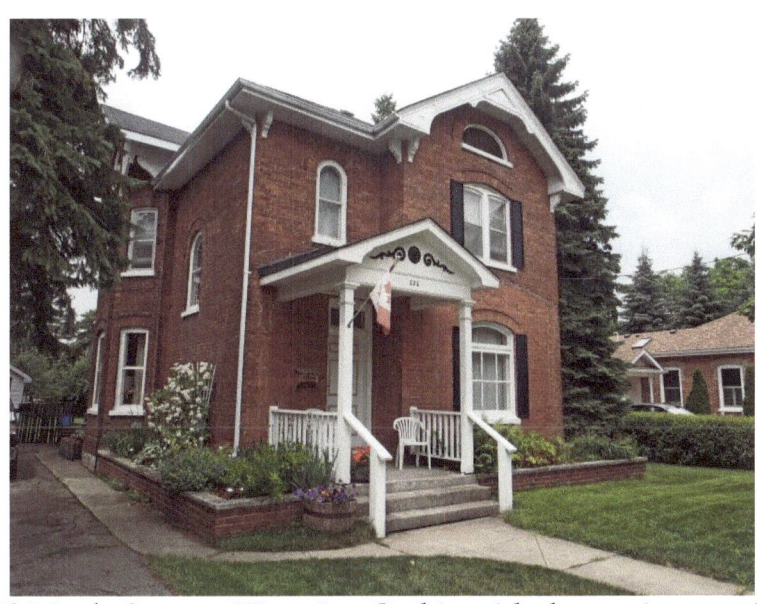

252 Maple Street – Victorian Gothic with decorative cornice brackets, verge board on gables

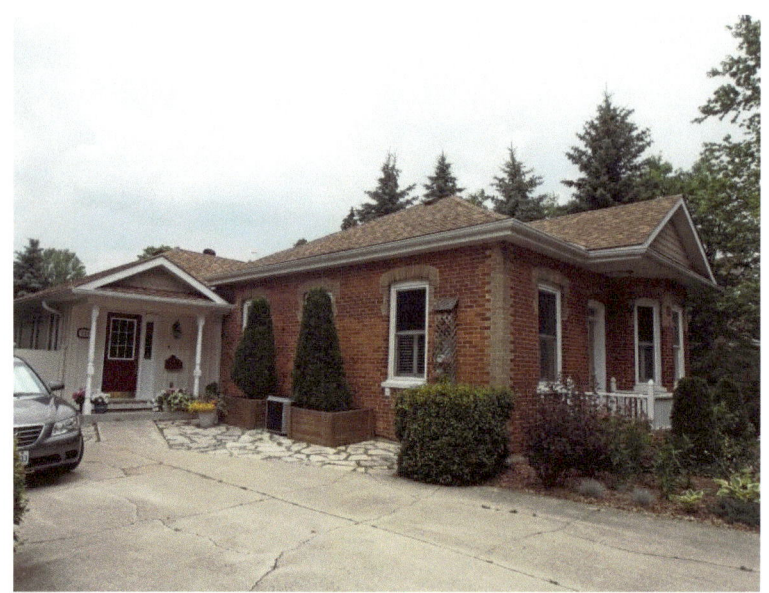

224 Maple Street - Regency Cottage with corner quoins

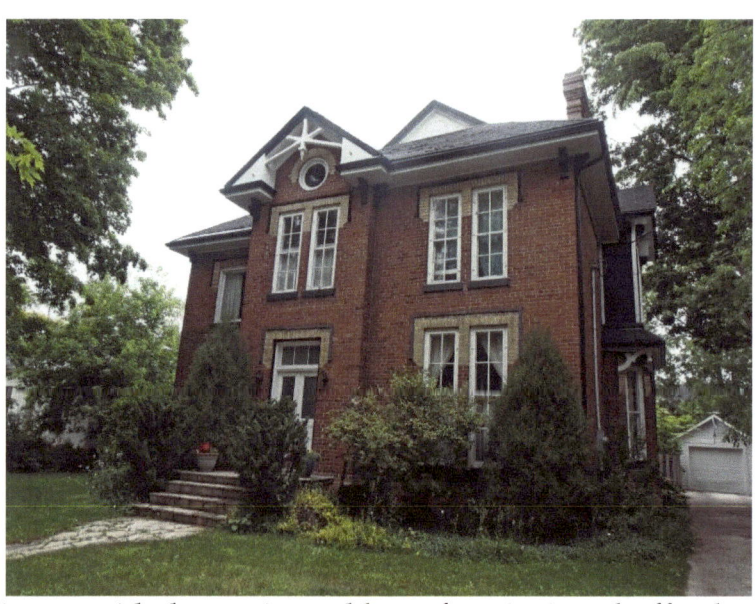

Italianate with decorative gable on frontispiece, buff-coloured window hoods

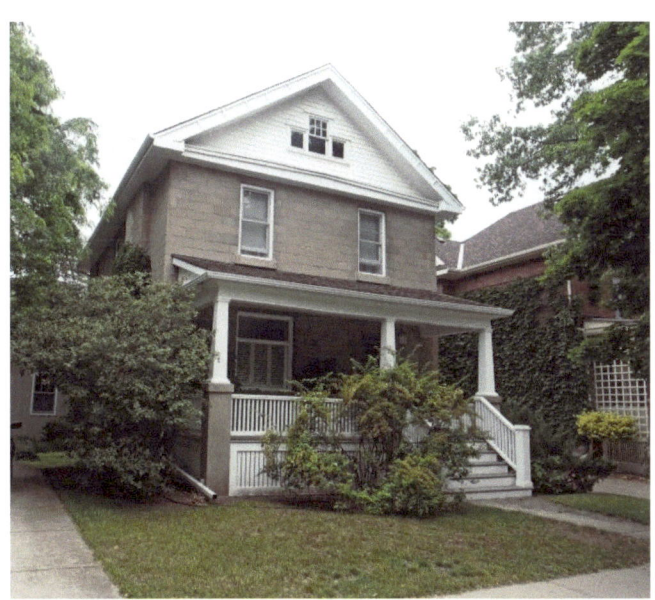

220 Maple Street - Edwardian style – Palladian window

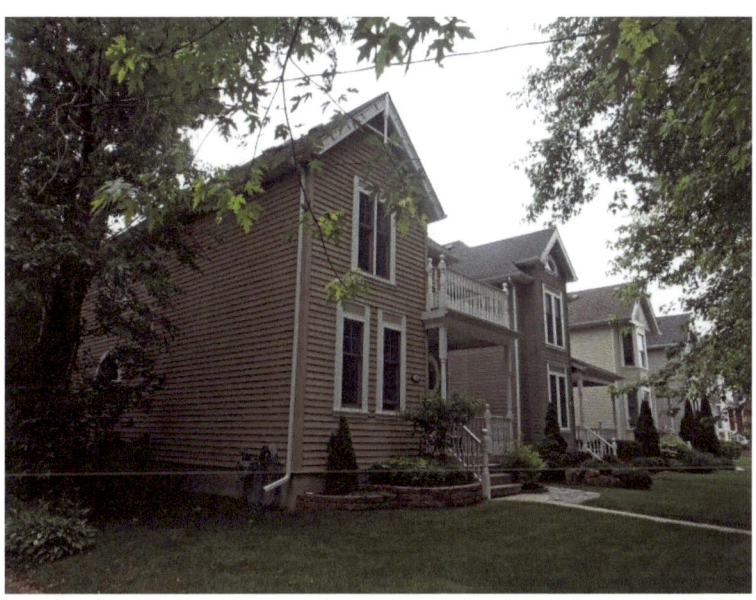

221 Maple Street – verge board trim on gable, second floor balcony

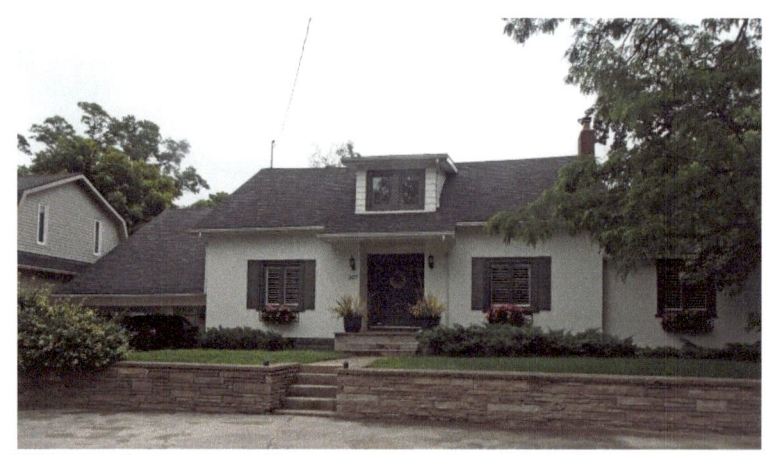

207 Maple Street – Regency cottage with dormer in attic

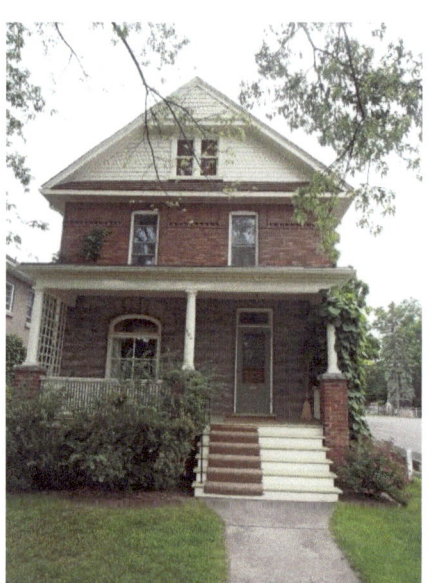

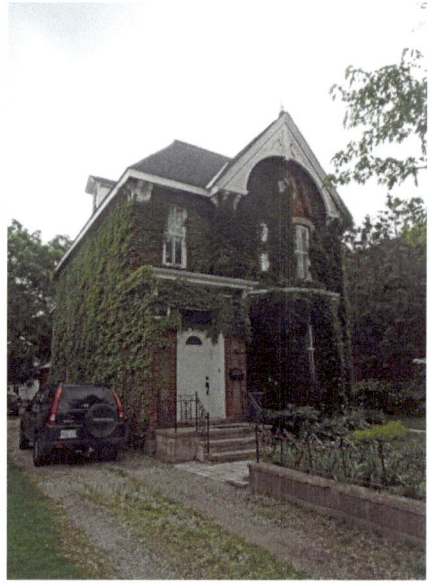

204 Maple Street
Edwardian style

125 Maple Street - vine covered Victorian Gothic style, verge board and finial on gable, dormer, and cornice brackets

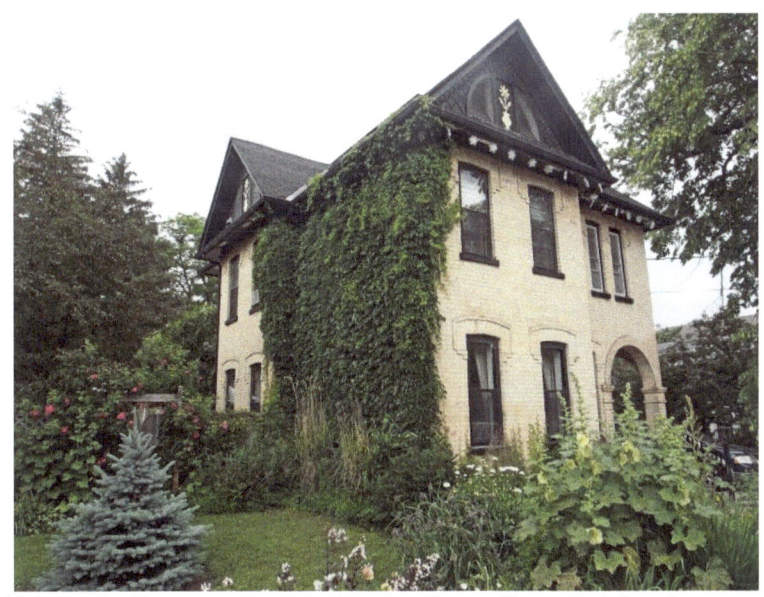

162 Maple Street - Gothic Revival – yellow brick, decorated tympanum, round arch, decorative window voussoirs

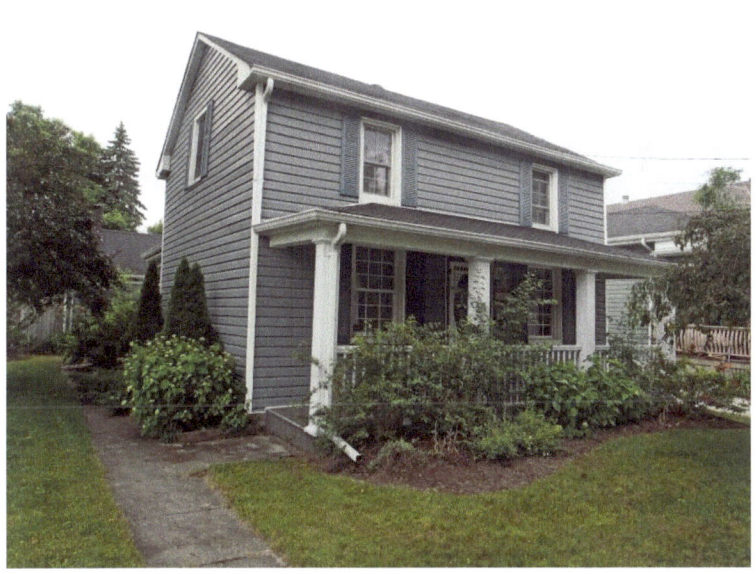

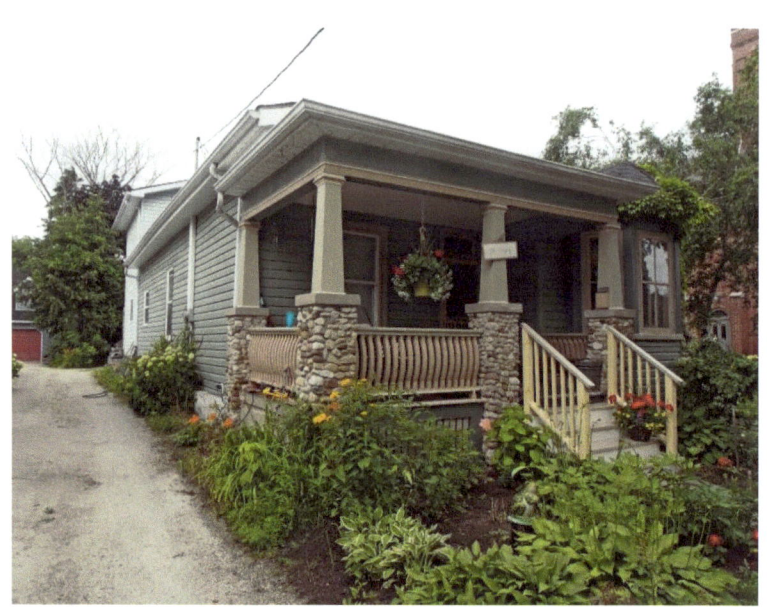

148 Maple Street - Regency Cottage

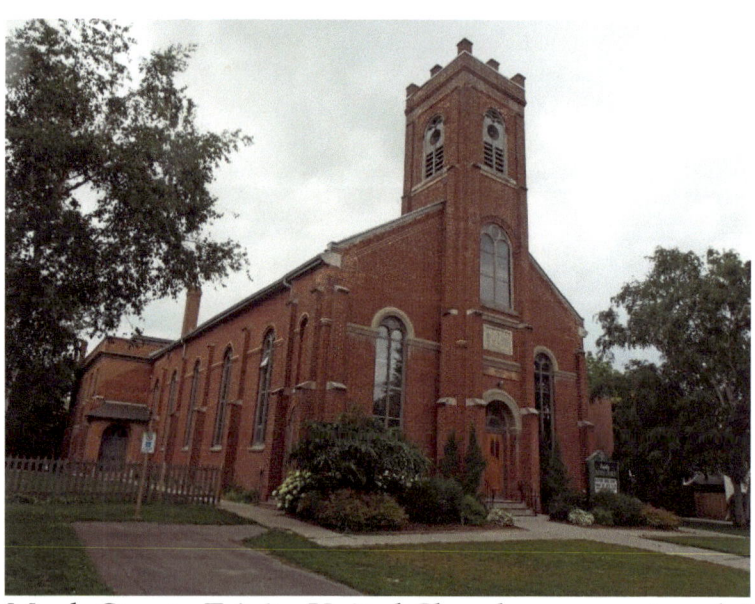

140 Maple Street - Trinity United Church – cornerstone laid in 1863 (Maple Street Methodist), Romanesque style, three-storey tower with battlement, buttresses

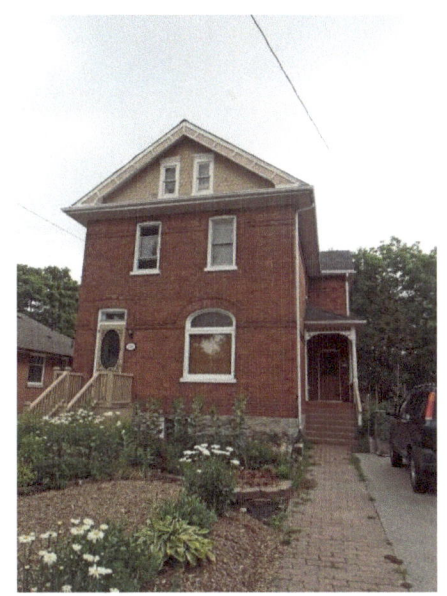

119 Maple Street – Edwardian style

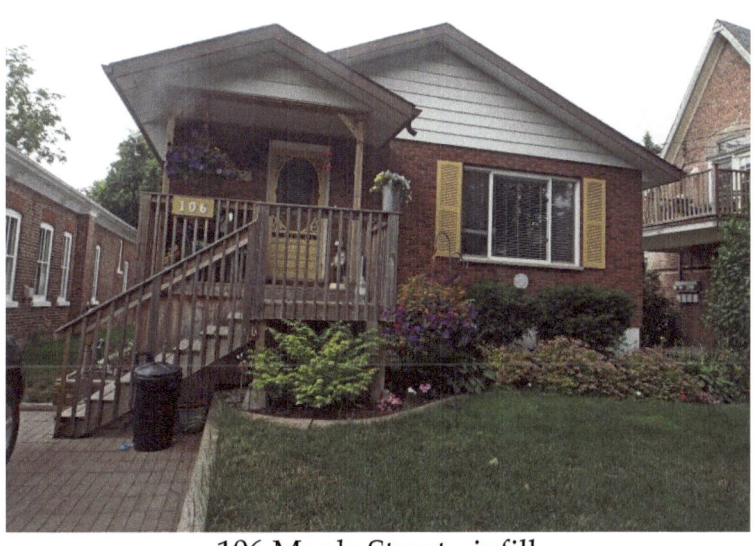

106 Maple Street - infill

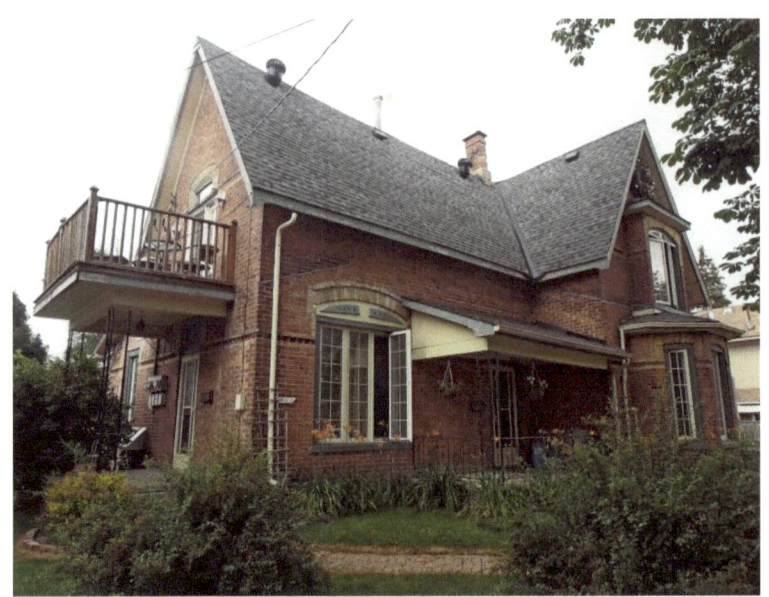

102 Maple Street – Gothic Revival – decorative arched window hoods, bay window, and second floor balcony

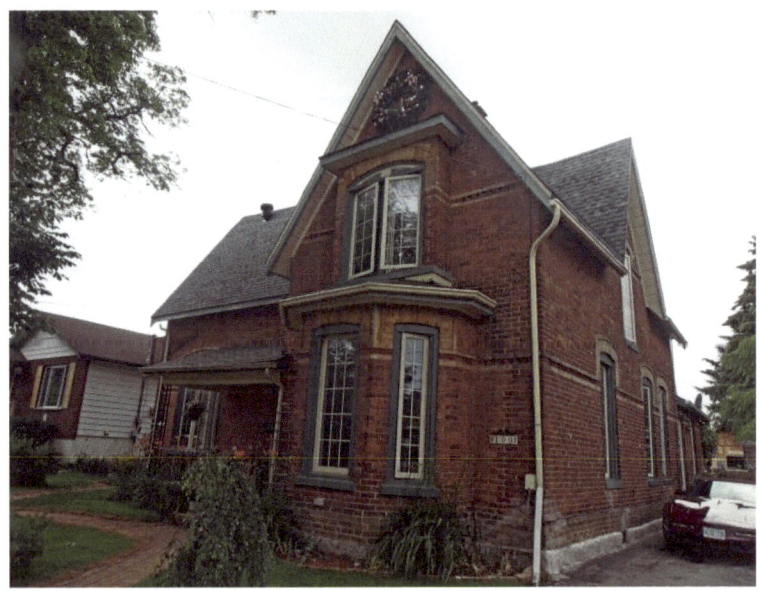

100 Maple Street – Gothic Revival, bay window, banding

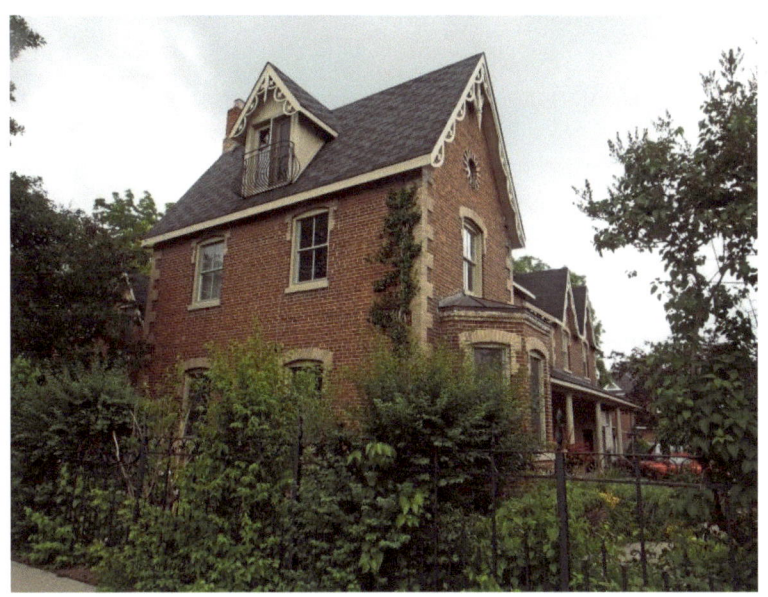

93 Maple Street - Gothic Revival

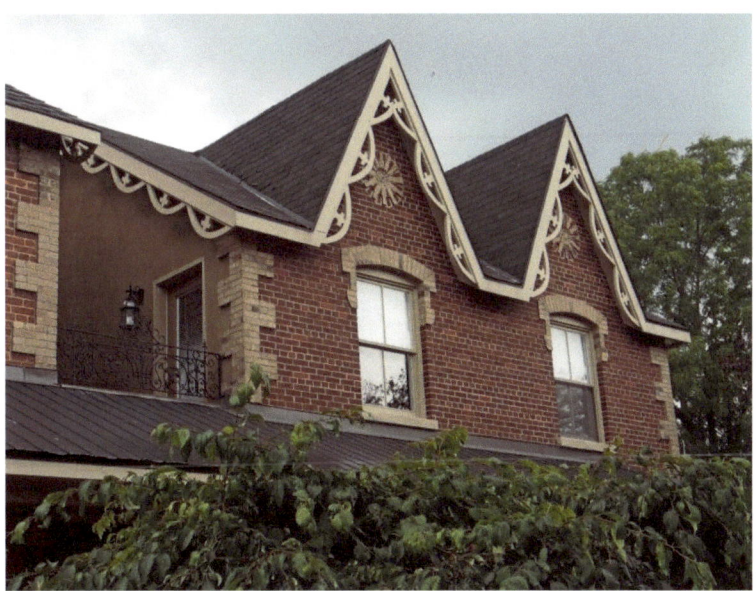

Decorative verge board trim on gables, finial, dichromatic brickwork and corner quoins

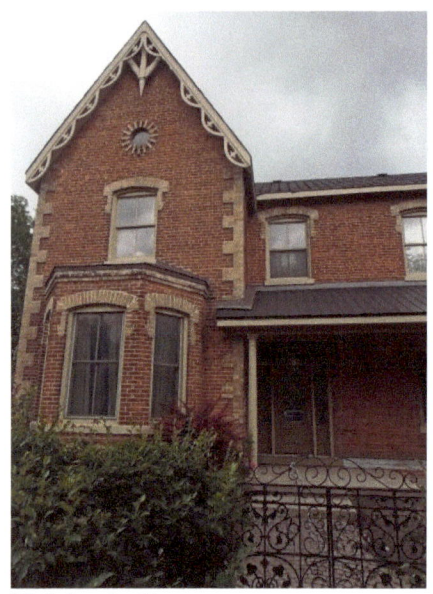
93 Maple Street

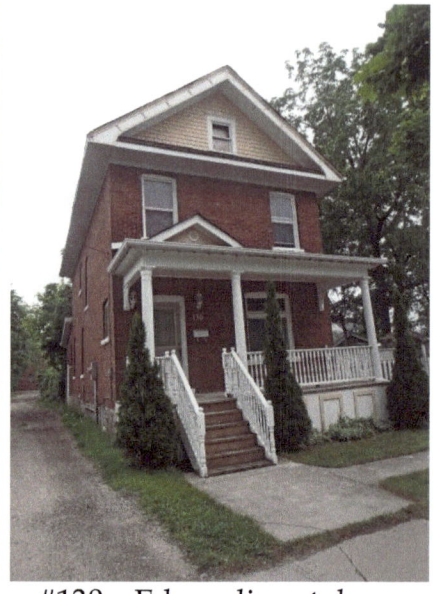
#130 – Edwardian style

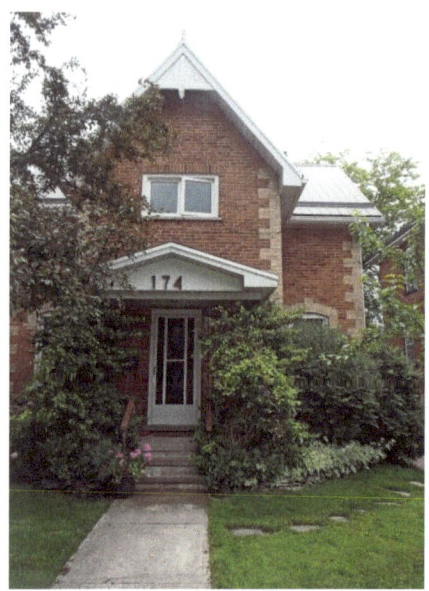
#174 – Gothic Revival dichromatic corner quoins

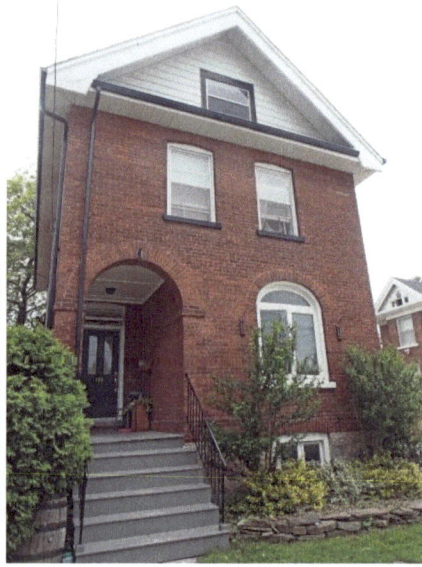
#180 – Edwardian style

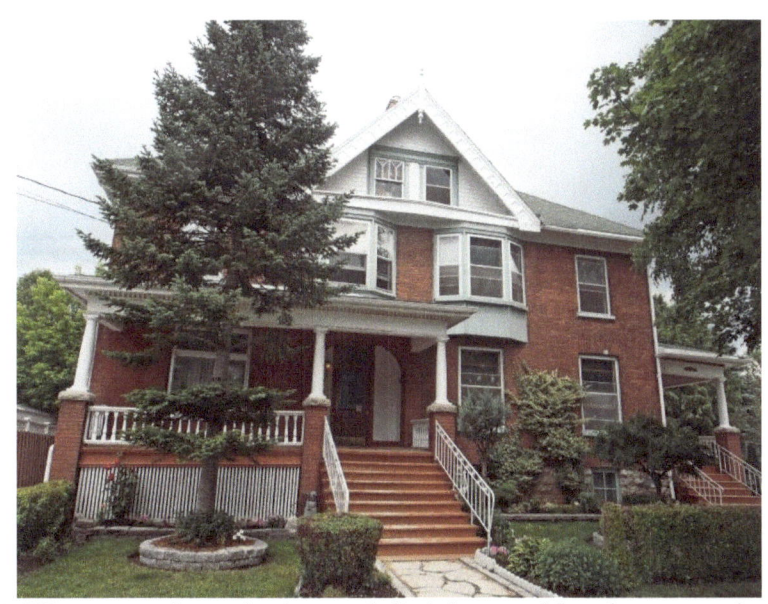

#175 – verge board trim and finial on gable, deep porches, second floor oriel windows

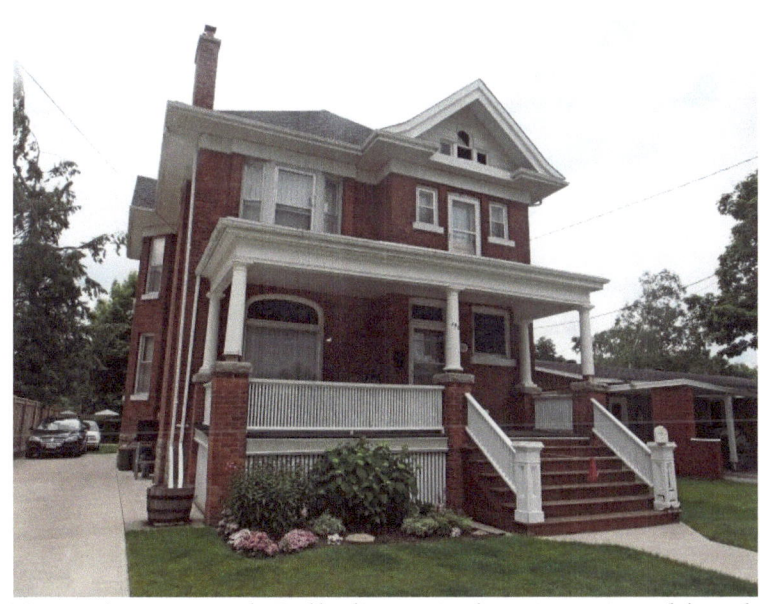

#190 – Italianate with Palladian window in attic gable which has cornice return

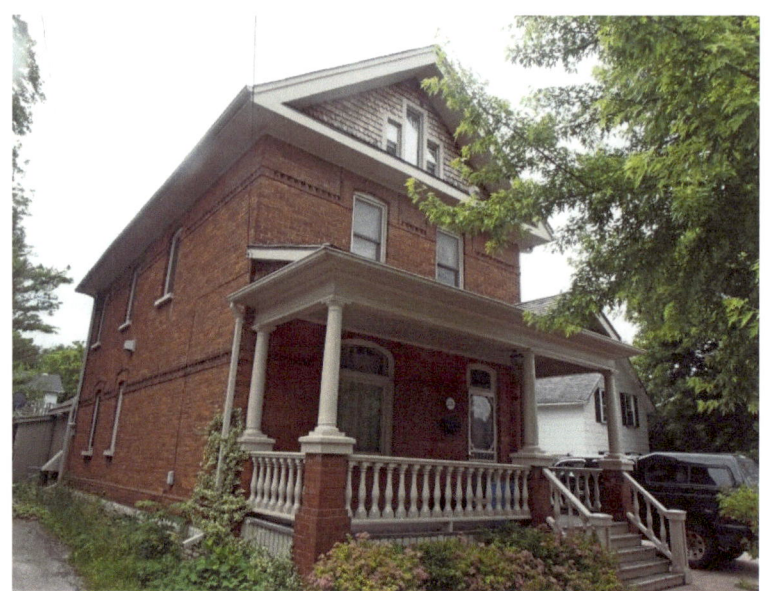

#224 - Edwardian style with Palladian window in gable

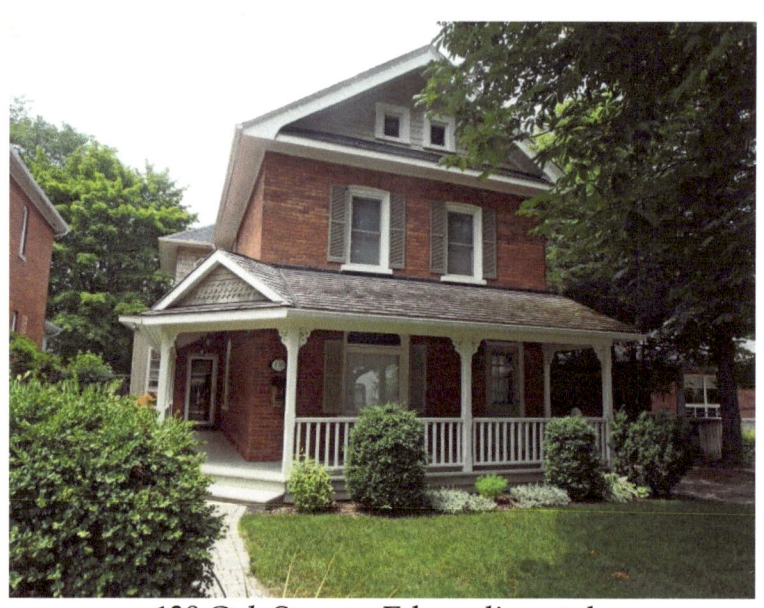

130 Oak Street – Edwardian style

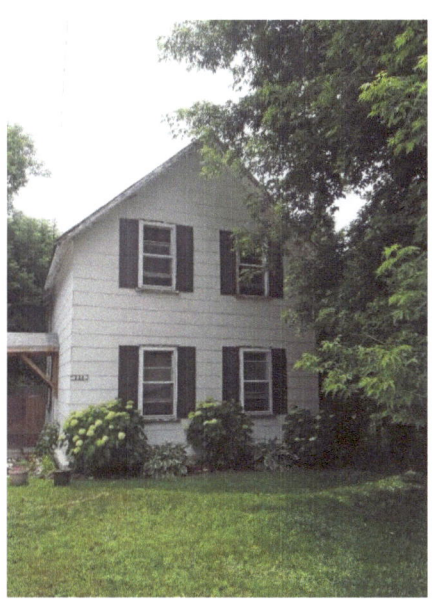
#228

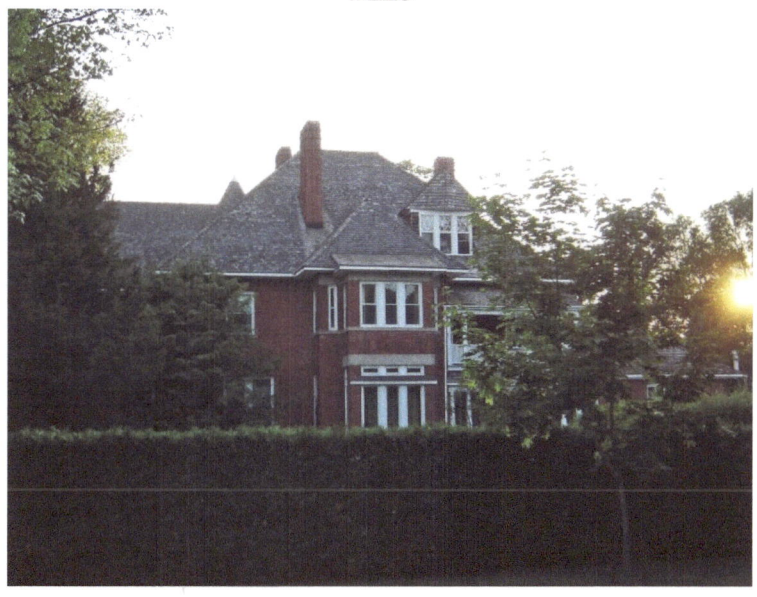

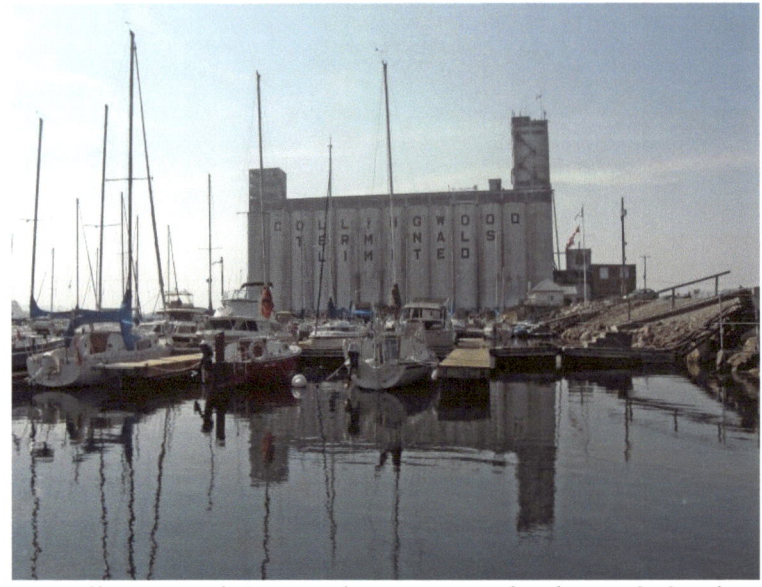

Collingwood Grain Elevator was built in 1919. The two million bushel grain elevator has bins 100 feet high and 22 feet in diameter. The steamer Munising arrived in September 1929 with 228,000 bushels of American grain, the first shipment for this important new structure. Grain shipments ended in 1993.

The arrival of the railroad in 1855 cemented Collingwood's worth as a center for shipping and shipbuilding as the rail line offered the ability to transport goods, materials and people easily and efficiently through the Great Lakes and points west.

Shipping by water meant that local wooden boat building flourished during the 1850s and 1860s. In addition to the activity in the harbor during navigation season, dozens of steamers wintered there every year. Following the completion of the Queen's Dry Dock at the foot of Hurontario Street in 1882, the corporate shipbuilding industry prospered. By the turn of the century, Collingwood was fast gaining an international reputation for consistent quality work and innovative design under the banner of the Collingwood Shipbuilding Company. Shipbuilding continued to play an important role in the fabric of the community's economy, with more than 1,000 employed during peak periods.

The shipyard, elevator and railroad continued to provide activity at the waterfront for many years until they were all deemed unprofitable by their owners and were terminated. The "Yard" closed in 1986 and the remaining shipyard buildings were removed in 1998. The remaining tracks were pulled up in 1997, and only the elevator remains, a reminder of Collingwood's once great harbor.

The Nottawasaga Island lighthouse, built in 1858, was one of six "imperial towers" built on the Great Lakes between 1855 and 1859. Contractor John Brown constructed the conical towers of dolomite limestone with walls 6' to 7' thick at the bottom and narrowing to 2' thick at the top. In order to support the French built cast iron polygonal lantern room, the limestone top was capped with granite. The Nottawasaga lighthouse towered 86' over the water and its revolving light was visible for seventeen miles. Manned by local keepers for 100 years, it was automated in 1959.

North West Mounted Police Departure Point, Collingwood

In October 1873, over 150 original members of the fledgling North-West Mounted Police (NWMP) gathered at Collingwood, Ontario on their way west to bring peace and order to the frontier. Mindful of the violence which had accompanied western expansion in the United States, Sir John A. MacDonald, Canada's first prime minister, conceived of NWMP to establish friendly relations with the aboriginal people and maintain the peace as settlers arrived.

The first members for this force were recruited in the provinces of Ontario and Quebec with some representation from the Atlantic Provinces. Most of these men had some previous military experience mainly in the Canadian Militia. They were transported by rail to the Port of Collingwood where they were issued with essential equipment in preparation for their journey to Lower Fort Garry in Manitoba via the Dawson route, an all Canadian way over land and water to the area of the Red River.

The first stage of the trip was by steamship from Collingwood to Prince Arthur's Landing (Thunder Bay). Collingwood is proud of its role in dispatching the first contingent of the NWMP to the frontier west at the beginning of the remarkable history of that force which in 1920 was renamed the Royal Canadian Mounted Police.

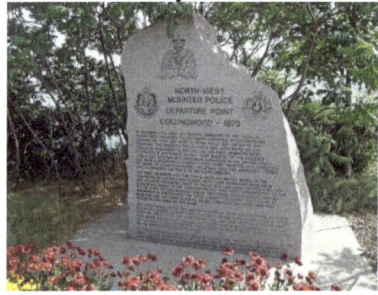
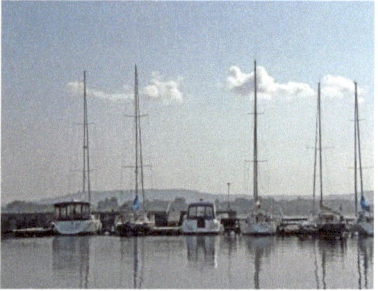
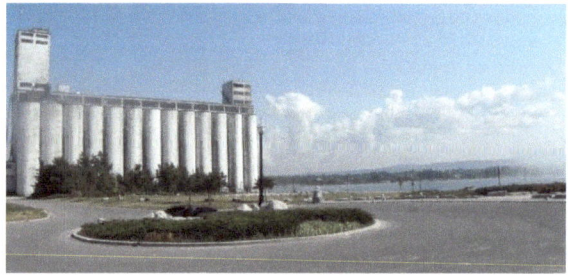

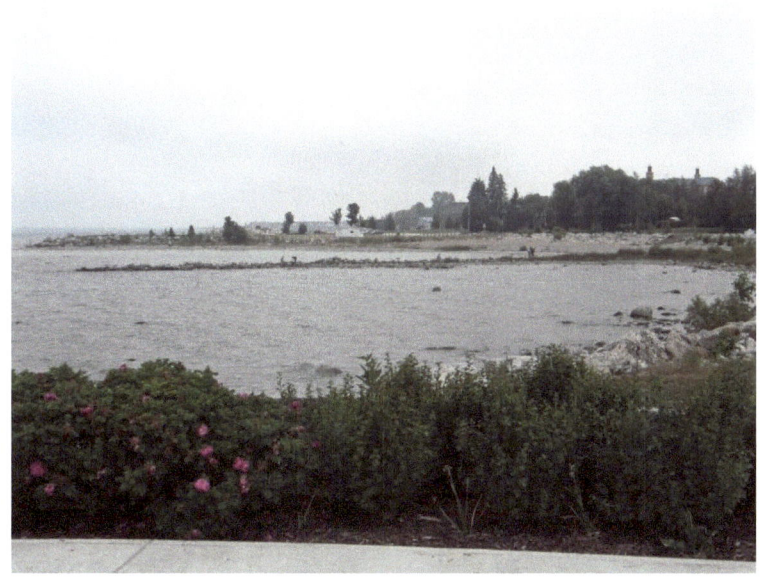

Sunset Point Beach, Collingwood, Ontario

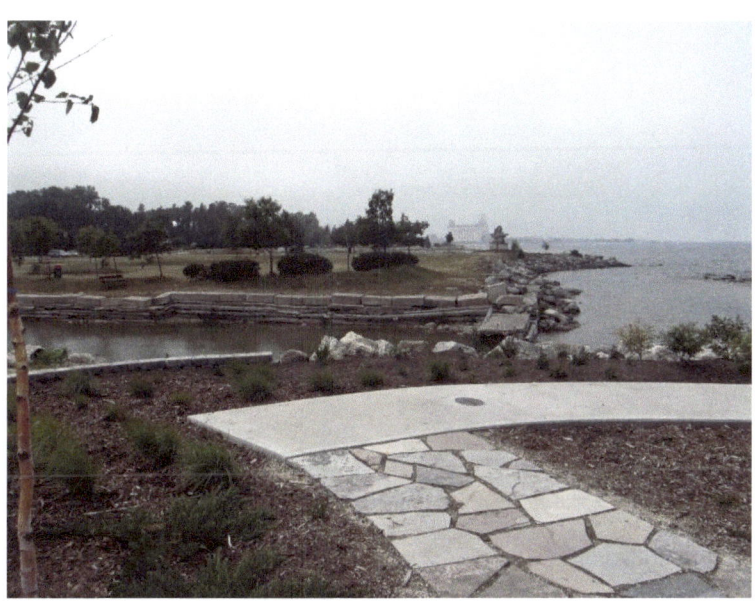

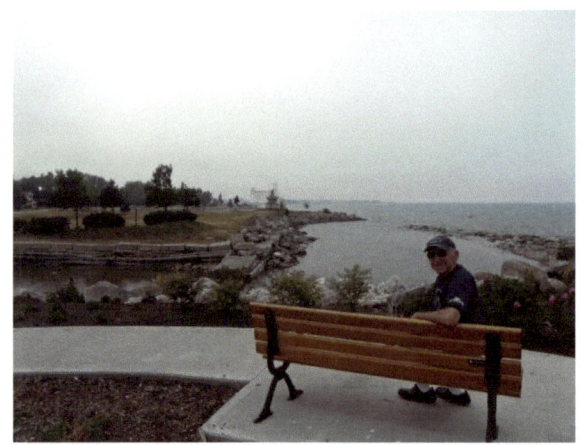

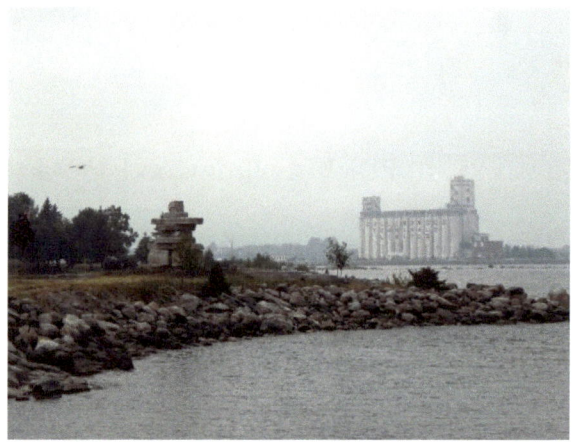

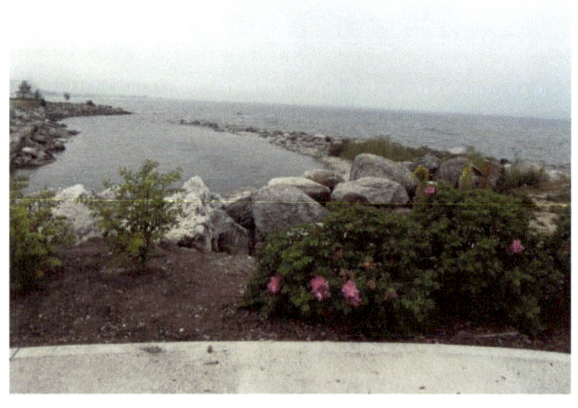

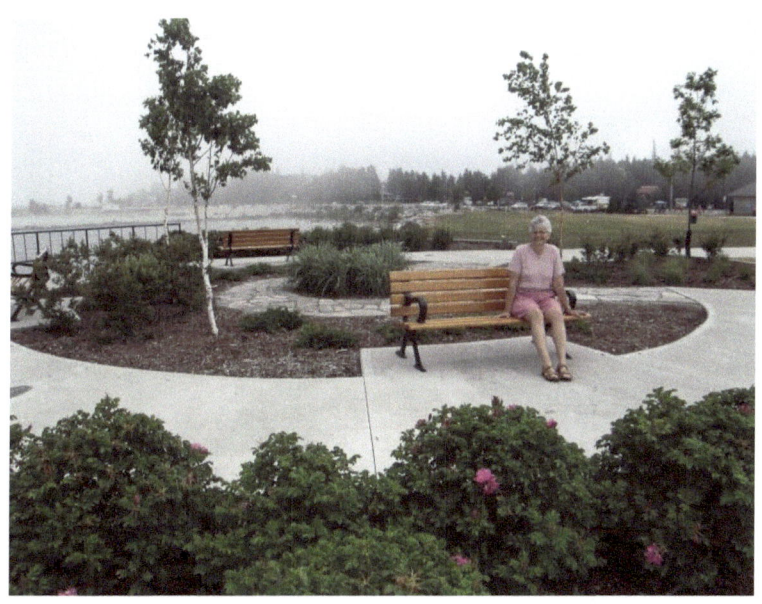

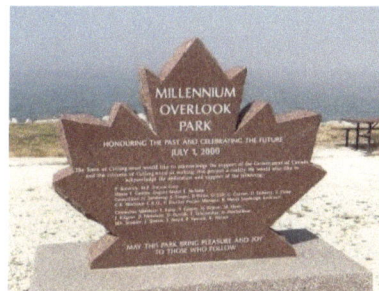 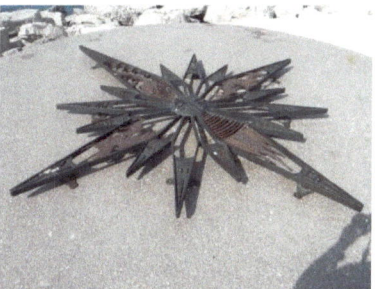

Millennium Overlook Park – honoring the past and celebrating the future

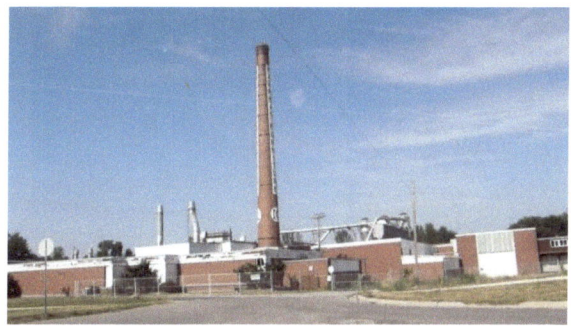

Kaufman Furniture Manufacturing – now closed

Architectural Terms

Brackets: a decorative or weight-bearing structural element which forms a right angle with one side against a wall and the other under a projecting surface such as an eave or roof. Example: Page 15	
Buttress: a masonry structure built against or projecting from a wall which serves to support or reinforce the wall. In Canadian architecture, they are sometimes used for decoration. Example: 200 Maple Street, Page 23	
Dentil Moulding: an even series of rectangles used as ornamental decoration in cornices. Example: Downtown building façade, Page 9	
Dichromatic brickwork: the use of two colours of brick, tile or slate to decorate a façade. Example: Downtown building façade, Page 6	
Dormer: (French for "sleep") a gable end window that pierces through the plane of a sloping roof surface to create usable space in the top floor or attic of a building by adding headroom. Example: 80 Third Street, Page 28	

Frontispiece: a portion of the façade of a building, usually a centred doorway that is slightly raised from the rest of the building, usually with white columned porches. Example: 203 Pine Street, Page 31	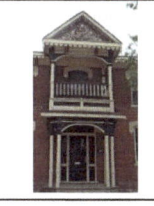
Gable: the triangular portion of a wall between the edges of a sloping roof. Example: Page 49	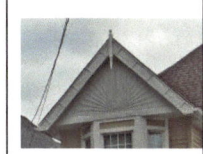
Hipped Roof: a roof where all sides slope downwards to the walls with no gables. Example: 90 Third Street, Page 27	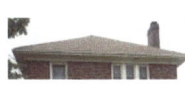
Keystones and Voussoirs: a voussoir is a wedge-shaped element used in building an arch. A keystone is the central stone that locks all the stones into position, allowing the arch to bear weight. A keystone is often enlarged and embellished. Example: 299 Maple Street, Page 45	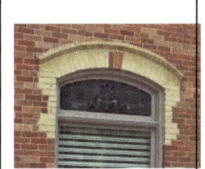
Lancet Window: a tall, narrow window with a pointed arch at its top. Example: 200 Maple Street, Page 23	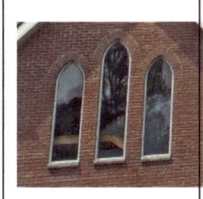

Palladian Window: a large window that is divided into three sections with the centre section larger than the two side sections and usually arched. Example: 206 Pine Street, Page 33	
Pediment: a triangular section above the horizontal structure (entablature), typically supported by columns. The inside of the triangle is called the tympanum. Example: 203 Pine Street, Page 31	
Quoin: masonry blocks at the corner of a wall, often a decorative feature, usually larger or of a different colour than the rest of the wall. Example: 302 Pine Street, Page 41	
Verge boards: also called bargeboards – hang from the projecting end of a roof and are often elaborately carved and ornamented. **Finial:** ornament added to the top of a gable – a Gothic element. Example: 242 Pine Street, Page 36	

Collingwood's Building Styles

Edwardian, 1900-1930 – This style bridges the ornate and elaborate styles of the Victorian era and the simplified styles of the 20th century, with balanced facades, simple roof lines, dormer windows, large front porches, and smooth brick surfaces. Example: 206 Pine Street, Page 33	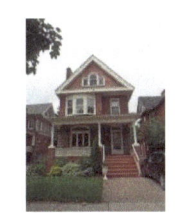
Georgian, before 1860 – These buildings have balanced facades around a central door, medium-pitched gable roofs, and small paned windows. Example: 258 Maple Street, Page 48	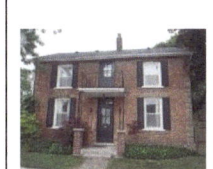
Gothic Revival, 1830-1890 – These decorative buildings have sharply-pitched gables with highly detailed verge boards, pointed-arch window openings, and dichromatic brickwork, a common style in Ontario. Example: 93 Maple Street, Page 58	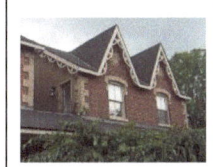
Italianate, 1850-1900 – It has wide-bracketed eaves, belvederes, wrap-around verandahs. Example: Page 15	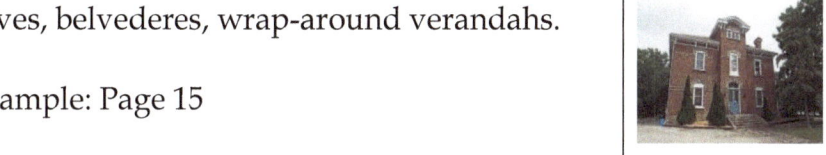
Queen Anne, 1885-1900 – This style has an irregular outline with a combination of an offset tower, broad gables, projecting two-storey bays, verandahs, multi-sloped roofs, and tall, decorative chimneys. Example: 276, 278 Pine Street, Page 42	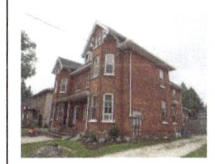

Neo-Classical, 1810-1850 – This style was a direct result of the War of 1812. Many Upper Canadians returning from the war with the United States were Loyalists who had inherited land from their forefathers. They had money and time to expand their holdings and indulge their architectural whims. Buildings were constructed on the traditional Georgian plan, but they had a new gaiety and light-heartedness. Detailing became more refined, delicate, and elegant. Example: 242 Third Street, Page 16	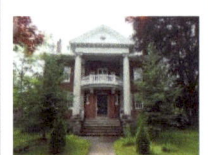
Regency Cottage, 1830-1860 – This style is a modest one-storey house with a low-pitched hip roof and has a symmetrical front façade. Example: Page 26	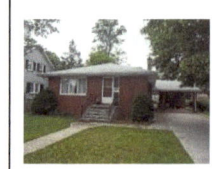
Romanesque Revival, 1880-1910 – This style hearkens back to medieval architecture of the 11th and 12th centuries with a heavy appearance, blocky towers and rounded arches. Example: 140 Maple Street, Page 57	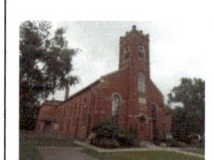
Victorian - In Ontario, a Victorian style building can be seen as any building built between 1840 and 1900 that doesn't fit into any of the other categories. It encompasses a large group of buildings constructed in brick, stone, and timber, using an eclectic mixture of Classical and Gothic motifs. Example: 200 Oak Street, Page 11	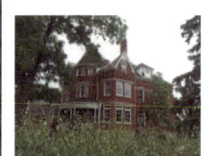

www.ingramcontent.com/pod-product-compliance
Lightning Source LLC
Chambersburg PA
CBHW040226220526
45473CB00001B/140